THE ATKINSON FILES, BEFORE DURING AND AFTER WWII
As told to Todd Slaughter

Resistance Mimeograph Machine

Cover art: Jon Aldersea

ISBN 9798312029390

Printing Machine used by Tony Atkinson to produce WW2 propaganda in occupied Europe

THE ATKINSON FILES, BEFORE DURING AND AFTER WWII

This work is not a biography but a story of "Tony Atkinson", a Nottinghamshire printer who during WWII performed some remarkable acts of bravery. Shot whilst trying to get aboard

evacuation boats on the beaches of Dunkirk, captured by the Germans, transferred to a military hospital in Holland before being cattle-trucked by train to a POW camp in Poland. His escape and a trek on foot across Poland, changing clothes with a dead German officer and walking into Luxembourg in the guise of Oberleutnant Anton Heidelberg, staying at Alfa Hotel and having breakfast with Lord Haw Haw. He helped to print propaganda materials for the resistance. I dedicate his recollections which he shared with me during the twenty years we worked together to his memory, and those my late father John Slaughter when he took my dad to see the brothels that he frequented in Paris during the war year, which are a feature in this work.

Other elements of this book recount the pop music and technical industry magazines that he printed. For Albert Hand Publications and The Robert Stigwood Organisation, these included Elvis Monthly, Fury Monthly, Mods Monthly, Teenbeat, Top Ten Hits, and Pop Weekly. For Todd Slaughter Productions the titles were Elvis Today, Rock Video, Cliff with The Kids in America, John Lennon Remembered, Elvis 25 Years A King, Satellite TV News, CB News, Pump News, 10-4 Action, Rastamag, Radio Luxembourg Club 208 magazine, Alvin Stardust Fanzine, Little & Large, plus the following annuals: Elvis Monthly, 10-4 Action and the Brian Clough Book of Football. In addition, the business enjoyed printing for celebrities who because of the Pop Weekly connection included Billy Fury, Joe Meek, Donovan, Ashley Kozak, Robert Stigwood and the infamous Doctor Steven Ward (Profumo / Mandy Rice-Davies / Christine Keeler). The English service of Radio Luxembourg played an important part of our lives, as it did to those readers who are still here and remember the station's broadcasts during the war years and throughout the second half of the 20th century.

I do not consider myself as an author – more a "storyteller", and for this story I refer to Tony Atkinson as "Anthony" throughout his war time adventure or his alter ego "Oberleutnant Anton Heidelberg". His full name being Anthony James Atkinson.

I had wanted to write a World War II book ever since I was a kid. Growing up in Leicester during the early days of television was certainly an adventure, and at home we got our first set just before the coronation of HM Queen Elizabeth II on 2 June 1953.

Walking to school at the age of six in 1951 I would pass the scorched earth where a German combat aircraft crashed and exploded. Even seven years after the Luftwaffe Junkers Ju88 burnt out on Stocking Farm, near where I lived in Leicester, there were still souvenirs: bits of metal, broken bakelite headphones and lots of tat.

In the '60s our TV existed on a diet of British WWII movies. We made the best war films, the American offerings, even today, concentrate the image of their super star actors forgetting the real story and of course in their films the GIs won every battle.

My Tony Atkinson stories rely on my memory of what he remembered about one of the greatest untold tales of his experiences in occupied Europe. I make no apologies for some creative writings where there were gaps in his recollections, and that also goes for the use of generic Polish, German and French names for the real characters in this work, who were not specified. Likewise, I was never given the names of the brave Luxembourg resistance members.

Tony's life after the war was just as interesting, and although he mixed with the rich, famous, and notorious, for the most part he was just "the anonymous printer" who rarely had his photograph taken. Tony was married twice. Initially to a lovely, divorced woman who already had a son Charles Hind. Lillian was a brilliant cook and home maker. After her death he remarried, this time to a Jewish lady who I never met. Tony Atkinson died in 1985 of prostate cancer and behind he left a life-long legacy of being one of the kindest guys on this planet. He helped and cared for everyone. The stories are unbelievable but please believe them even if the timeline is a little flaky. To enhance the scenes of the time I've included some of the WWII campaigns, but this book is not to be considered as a history lesson. Let "The Great Escape" do that. I asked actor John Leyton what he got paid every time that movie is on TV. "No royalties we got wages. The big earners were Attenborough, McQueen, Bronson, Pleasence and Garner."

Todd Slaughter

Todd Slaughter seen here riding Elvis' tandem around the streets of Luxemburg with 208 DJ Peter Aldersley in 1970. A publicity picture for the MGM movie "Elvis: That's The Way It Is." (Picture courtesy of MGM producer Dennis Sanders.) Todd is better known as being the honorary president of the Official Elvis Presley Fan Club, but he is also an author, writer, publisher, broadcaster and mechanical engineer. He was the person who within hours of Telstar (the first communications satellite) being launched in 1962, saw the possibility of this space vehicle being used not only for telemetry, radio and TV news gathering but for live entertainment. He announced his plans and thoughts to the press and conceived the idea for Elvis Presley to appear on TV direct from the USA to around the world once the technology had been perfected. Ten years later Elvis Presley announced that he would be appearing globally, live from Honolulu, accessible to every country in the world is a show which was to be named "Elvis: Aloha from Hawaii". Over the years Todd Slaughter has written, edited and published a variety of books and magazines including consumer entertainment titles, fanzines, mechanical and electrical engineering journals and even a football annual about which he knew nothing about. As a journalist he supplied pieces to domestic and overseas newspapers and has broadcast regularly on British and foreign radio and television services.

"The Atkinson Files" is a true and previously untold story about a WWII soldier, and it also includes personal life stories about Slaughter's biological parents and adopted mum and dad.

Throughout this book there are ongoing references to Radio Luxembourg and the influence that this totally legal media giant had before, during and after the war. Their English language radio services were never jammed across Eastern Europe and Radio Luxembourg was *the* radio station with a diet of popular music culture which was helping millions of oversea listeners to learn the English language.

Sunday, May 5 to Saturday, May 11, 1935.

PROGRAMMES

from the

CONTINENT in ENGLISH

Information supplied by International Broadcasting Co. Ltd., 11, HALLAM STREET, PORTLAND PLACE, LONDON, W.1   *Copyright Reserved.*

Sunday, May the Fifth

All Times stated are British Summer Time

PARIS (Poste Parisien)
312 metres, 959 Kc/s., 100 kW.

Announcer : J. Sullivan.
Afternoon Programme

5.0 p.m.

WALTZES BY STRAUSS

Roses of the South.
Viennese Bonbons.
Du and du (Die Fledermaus).
Voices of Spring.

5.15 p.m.

SYLVAN SWEETHEARTS

Popular Songs of Love and Romance

Signature Tune.
Whisper Sweet ... ... Trent
Hands Across the Table ... ... Parish
When Day is Done ... ... Katcher
Like a Doll from the Blue ... Oakland
Nobody's Sweetheart Now ... ... Kahn
Special Orchestrations by Van Phillips.

*Programme Production by
Universal Programmes Corporation, Ltd.*

For mountains of rich, creamy lather use Sylvan Soap Flakes—giant size box for 1s.

5.30 p.m.

STRANG'S FOOTBALL POOLS
BROADCAST
VARIETY

Commonityland Selection.
On the Other Side of the Hill ... Kennedy
Green Meadows ... ... Lenn
Sailing up the Clyde ... ... Fyffe
For Love Alone.
Selection—Florodora ... ... Stuart
You Bring Out the Savage in Me ... Coslow
In Town To-night ... ... Coslow

Strang's 2d. Pool constantly breaks its own records. Particulars from Strang's Football Pools, Hawkhill Avenue, Edinburgh 7.

6.0 p.m.

ALMOND EYES

Japanese Lantern Dance ... ... Yoshimoto
Chinatown, My Chinatown ... ... Jerome
One Fine Day (Madame Butterfly) ... Puccini
Chinese Street Serenade ... ... Siede

6.15 p.m.

BART SHARP'S VARIETY CONCERT

Signature Tune.
Harry Lauder Selection.
That Handsome Accordian Man ... Box
Il Winter Comes ... ... Billy Bennet

Write for football coupons to Bart Sharp & Co., Ltd., Liverpool—the firm with the long tradition.

6.30 p.m.

PIANO RECITAL

Valse in A Flat Op. 69 No. 1 ... ... Chopin
Melody in F ... ... Rubinstein
Rhapsody in E Flat 4 ... ... Brahms
Slavonic Dances ... ... Dvorak

(Continued on page 25, column 1)

RADIO LUXEMBOURG
1304 metres, 230 Kc/s., 200 kW.

Announcers : S. H. C. Williams and Gerald Carnes.
12 (Noon)
BOBBIE COMBER & REGINALD PURDELL
in the
MUSICAL VOYAGE
EPISODE NO. 4
Halls Wine strengthens you when tired or run down.

12.15 p.m.

DO-DO BROADCASTS
Asthma Sufferers ! For the quickest and cheapest relief take Do-Do Asthma Tablets. Send 1½d. stamp for a generous test sample to : International Laboratories, 100 Smedley Street, London, S.W.8.

12.30 p.m. THE IRISH CONCERT
GOLDEN HOUR OF MUSIC
A Symphony in rich and glorious melody . . . a rhapsody of tuneful song
*Programme Production by
Universal Programmes Corporation, Ltd.*

OUR JUBILEE PROGRAMMES

This week all thoughts are centred on the King's Jubilee, and on Sunday and Monday the I.B.C. presents the following special Jubilee Programmes.

RADIO NORMANDY

Sunday.	10.0 a.m.	JUBILEE PARADE
	10.30 p.m.	LOOKING BACKWARDS.
Monday.	8.15 a.m.	JUBILEE PROCESSION.
	5.15 p.m.	REMINISCENCES—1910 TO 1935.
	11.0 p.m.	JUBILEE MEMORIES.

RADIO LUXEMBOURG

Monday.	6.15 p.m.	JUBILEE THOUGHTS.

PARIS (Poste Parisien)

Monday.	10.30 p.m.	TWENTY-FIVE YEARS—A JUBILEE REVIEW.

1.0 p.m. ZAM-BUK BROADCAST
Of the Latest Dance Music
Keep a tin of Zam-Buk in your home and be ready with a safe treatment for cuts, burns and bruises.

1.30—2.0 p.m.
LITTLEWOOD'S BROADCAST
Give yourself a chance to be among the lucky prizewinners in Littlewood's Football Pools next week. Coupons from H. Littlewood, Ltd., Liverpool.

2.30—3.0 p.m. VERNON'S
ALL-STAR VARIETY CONCERT
(Gramophone Records)

Signature Tune.
Life Begins at Oxford Circus
Jack Hylton and his Orchestra.
Old Fashioned Love. (The Mills Brothers.)
One Night of Love. (Gracie Fields.)
She Wore a Little Jacket of Blue.
Jack Hylton and his Orchestra.
Another One Gone. (Norah Blaney and Gwen Farrar.)
Pop Goes Your Heart ... ... Dixon
Bobbie Howes.
Songs from the Shows. (Arranged by John Watt.)
Vernon's Football Pool Coupon means an opportunity of sharing in very substantial dividends. Write : Vernon's Pools, Liverpool.

(Continued on page 24, middle of column 4)

RADIO NORMANDY
269.5 metres, 1113 Kc/s.

Announcers : C. Danvers-Walker, A. Campbell and E. J. Osterman.

8.15 a.m.

ECHOES OF SPAIN

Picador ... ... Morris
Spanish Love ... ... Bazzo
Lady of Spain ... ... Groser
Toreador Song ... ... Bizet
I.B.C. Time Signal.
Spanish Gipsy Dance ... ... Marquina
Señorita Carmencita ... ... Spoliansky
Valencia ... ... Padilla
El Turia—Spanish Waltz ... ... Granado

8.45 a.m.

SONGS AT THE PIANO

Hands Across the Table ... ... Parish
Tina ... ... Kennedy
Must I Go On Like This ? ... ... Lawnhurst
I've Brought You Some Narcissus Co ... Morris

9.0 a.m.

LIGHT MUSIC

The Count of Luxembourg Waltz ... Lehar
When Day is Done ... ... de Sylva
La Rosita ... ... Dupont
Indigestion sufferers—for your health's sake insist on genuine Maclean Brand Stomach Powder.
Sons of the Sand ... ... Noble
Mandy ... ... Berlin
Eastern Medley.
She doesn't need to ask for " Outside line " now.
She's 'phoning while she sleeps—with nightly doses of Bile Beans.
Waltz Romantique ... ... de Costa
The Ants' Parade ... ... Rakke

9.30 a.m. " RADIO PICTORIAL "
CELEBRITY CONCERT
(Gramophone Records)
Signature Tune—You Oughta be in Pictures.
Sing 'em Again Selection.
Primo Scala's Accordion Band.
I Love the Moon (Un Grand Trio.) ... Bohaus
John Watt's Songs from the Films—The Three Little Pigs.
My Old Dog (Patriot Collier) ... ... Sarony
Charlie Kunz Medley No. 3. (Charlie Kunz.)
Lonely Heart (Patricia Rossborough.) ... Brelin
Down at Our Charity Bazaar ... ... Ase
Gracie Fields.

Your newsagent can supply you with " Radio Pictorial "—the paper that keeps you in touch with the broadcasting world.

10.0 a.m. ORCHESTRAL MUSIC
Stephanie Gavotte ... ... Czibulka
When the Lemons Bloom ... ... Strauss
It is easy on the carton " made by Maclean, Ltd., Gt. West Road, London," it's genuine Maclean Brand Stomach Powder.
Violin Solo—Valse, Op 80 ... ... Brahms
Gold and Silver Waltz ... ... Lehar

10.15 a.m. BALLITO CONCERT
DANCE MUSIC
Signature Tune—Happy Feet.
A Little White Gardenia—Fox trot ... Coslow
Believe It, Beloved—Fox trot ... ... Johnston
When My Prince Charming Comes Along ... Coslow
Just Once Too Often—Fox trot ... ... Sieg
Ballito Pure Silk Stockings are sold by good drapers everywhere—ask to see the new season's colours.

(Continued on page 24, column 1)

SYLVAN SWEETHEARTS sing you songs of love and romance. Listen to them to-day from RADIO LUXEMBOURG (1304 m.) at 3.15 p.m., PARIS (Poste Parisien), 312 m., at 5.15 p.m., and RADIO NORMANDY (269.5 m.) at 6.30 p.m.   23

INTRODUCTION

Operation Dynamo was the code name given to the evacuation of allied soldiers hemmed in by German forces in May 1940. Lined up on the Dunkirk beaches over half a million men were waiting for a place on a flotilla of unlikely vessels to get them back to Blighty. Seaside pleasure boats, trawlers, out of commission freighters and ships of all shapes and sizes were pressed ganged into service crewed by volunteers including under-age school kids and pensioners who had a smattering of experiences in matters maritime.

Dunkirk went very well. Churchill was lucky, and the fact that it coincided with his arrival as Prime Minister meant that the British public felt that they now had a saviour. Astonishingly some 350,000 British and French soldiers reached the safety of the White Cliffs of Dover, though 40,000 Brits were killed during their attempted escape, and a further 100,000 were captured and sent to Nazi POW Camps in all countries now occupied by the Germans. Initial treatments to some of those captured was barbaric. Brutalities were metered out even as Dunkirk was being evacuated.

On 28 May 1940 the SS Totenkopf Division marched about 100 members of the 2nd Battalion of the Royal Norfolk Regiment, which had just surrendered, to a pit in a farm in Le Paradis and murdered them with machine gun spray. A similar atrocity unfolded on the same day with the 2nd Battalion of the Royal Warwickshire Regiment, which had been captured near Wormhoudt, in France. They were forced into a barn and massacred with grenades. As the war dragged on, forced marches became more common, sometimes with very little food or none. One British battalion reported receiving only two sugar lumps and two tablespoons of a mixture of carrots and potatoes a day. On arriving at train stations, the POWs were loaded into cattle cars for trips to work sites in Germany and Poland.

The Geneva Convention rules, which lay out protections and standards of treatment of POWs; were not always followed, but generally the Germans behaved fairly towards British and Commonwealth prisoners. Even so, conditions were tough. Rations were meagre. The men, but not officers, had to work, often at heavy labour. The days dragged and there was a constant battle against boredom. Prisoners tried to overcome this by staging entertainments and educating themselves. Contrary to the popular myth, most men were too weak from hunger and work to try to escape. Those who did get beyond the wire ran the very real risk of being shot. Germany was a signatory to the Third Geneva Convention of 1929, which itemised the rules relating to the treatment of prisoners of war. Article 10 required POWs be lodged in adequately heated and lighted buildings where conditions were the same as for German troops. Articles 27-32 detailed the conditions of labour.

Enlisted ranks were required to perform whatever labour they were asked if able to do, so long as it was not dangerous and did not support the German armaments war-effort. Senior non-commissioned officers (sergeants and above) were required to work only in a supervisory role. Commissioned officers were not required to work, although they could volunteer. The work performed was largely agricultural or industrial, ranging from coal or potash mining, stone quarrying, or work in sawmills, breweries, factories, railroad yards and forests. POWs hired out to military and civilian contractors were supposed to receive pay and get at least one day a week of rest. Article 76 ensured that POWs who died in captivity were honourably buried in marked graves. The British POW's held in German camps were run by the military and enjoyed a tolerable time and the Red Cross had reasonable access to the camps. German POW camps were usually run fairly. As the men in these camps were from the military and generally former German military personnel ran these camps, there was a degree of empathy between both sides.

The British government had made it clear that they expected British POWs to try to escape and the Germans would have been aware of this, especially as German POWs in Britain were also expected to do likewise. The delicate balance between captive and captor was only usually broken by an intervention by the SS. Cases of poor treatment of prisoners by the military staff at a German POW camp were rare, though they undoubtedly existed. So-called "goon bating" was rare as it would only serve to antagonise those who worked in the camps and make life for the POWs even more difficult. The Red Cross was usually given good access to German POW camps with prisoners receiving Red Cross parcels from families, friends, the churches and charities together with communication between families at home and POW's in Germany. This operated as good as it could have been given the circumstances of war.

A British squaddie was of little interest to the Gestapo as most soldiers had little or no idea where they were during their time in the "theatres of war" or for that matter what the objectives were, except on a day-to-day basis. They had little or no knowledge of any masterplans and although never considered as "cannon fodder" there were no secrets to uncover, so they were not as closely guarded as air crew and pilots.

Captured RAF flyers, navigators and surveillance personnel were valuable to the SS, but their incarcerators were overseen by injured or retired officers of the Luftwaffe. The Luftwaffe tended to treat their POWs very well because they knew that the Allies had many of their men held as prisoners in the UK, so any word of poor treatment was likely, they thought, to be responded with similar actions on the other side. There was a strong sense of chivalry between the British RAF and German Luftwaffe pilots; they liked to regard themselves as "knights of the air" and shooting defenceless enemy pilots in their parachutes would be contrary to their pilots' professionalism.

In some camps Army POWs were given opportunities to go into the nearby communities to shop or barter with the locals though they were prohibited from going into places where alcohol was consumed or sold. "Flyers" however were never allowed to go beyond their barbed wired electric fenced penitentiaries, overseen from machine-gunned and searchlight encrusted observation towers.

Our story is about a British Army Private who we will call during this true-life adventure "Anthony". What Tony Atkinson told me about his experiences during and after the war is truthful and remarkable. To his advantage was his scholarly knowledge of languages and being educated by Jesuit priests he excelled in and spoke good German, French and a smattering of Spanish. He kept his linguistic skills to himself not wishing to be assigned to tasks within the Army which might shorten his life. "I am a little fella, and I didn't wish to get any shorter than my 5' 4" stature."

Anthony's education took place at St Patrick's - this new school for Senior Boys was built at Sneinton Dale and opened in 1933. It was dedicated to St Bernadette (who had just been canonised that year). The site on Sneinton Dale was bought by a legacy left by Miss Elizabeth Atkin, a cleaner at Boots', who had devoted her whole life to the parish. Young Tony left school aged 15 in 1935. Academically the young man could have qualified for a bursary for higher education and then gone on to university, but his father died in a freak accident a year earlier in Hucknall Colliery.

CHAPTER ONE

THE WAR CRY

WEEKLY GUARDIAN
The Popular Illustrated Weekend Paper with its Original and Attractive Local Features
Every Friday Morning 1d.

Nottingham Evening Post

FOOTBALL POST
Most Results
Best Reports
and Pictures

No. 19,079.   SUNDAY, SEPTEMBER 3, 1939.   PAGES   ONE PENNY

BRITAIN AT WAR WITH GERMANY
Premier's Momentous Statement In The Commons

MR. CHAMBERLAIN'S FINAL WORDS

"I Trust I May Live To See Hitlerism Destroyed"

FATEFUL DAY IN WORLD'S HISTORY

IN A MOMENTOUS SPEECH IN THE HOUSE OF COMMONS TO-DAY, THE PRIME MINISTER DECLARED THAT THIS COUNTRY WAS NOW AT WAR WITH GERMANY.

THE PREMIER'S VOICE TREMBLED AS HE SAID: "EVERYTHING THAT I HAVE WORKED FOR, EVERYTHING THAT I HAVE HOPED FOR, EVERYTHING THAT I BELIEVED IN DURING MY PUBLIC LIFE HAS CRASHED INTO RUINS THIS MORNING.

"There is only one thing left for me, and that is to devote what strength and powers I have to forwarding the victory of the cause for which we have to sacrifice ourselves.

The Premier's final words were, "I cannot tell what part I may be allowed to play myself. I trust I may live to see the day when Hitlerism has been destroyed and a restored and liberated Europe has been re-established."

No Replies Received

A Changed Atmosphere

Britain's Determination

Poland's Restraint

Aerial Warfare Question

Saving World From Nazi Tyranny

Tribute Of Sympathy To Premier

Fighting For Very Existence

"This Horrible Catastrophe"

THE MEN OF THE MOMENT

THE KING'S MESSAGE TO THE EMPIRE

"Stand Calm, Firm And United"

NOTTM. SCHOOLS CLOSED

Nottingham Lord Mayor's Appeal

HITLER'S CHOICE

Refusal Of The British Demands

"NO INTENTION TO ANNIHILATE POLAND"

Premier's Proclamation

EVACUATING NOTTINGHAM

WAR CABINET CONSTITUTED
Mr. Churchill First Lord Of Admiralty

His mother, a "tea-lady" at the Nottingham Evening Post, heard that the newspaper was interviewing for the position of an apprentice compositor in the print room. So, she asked if her son could apply. During much of the letterpress era, movable type was composed by hand for each page by workers called compositors. A tray with many dividers, called a case, contained cast metal *sorts*, each with a single letter or symbol, but backwards (so they would print correctly). The compositor assembled these sorts from a variety of font sizes and styles into words, then lines, then pages of text, which were then bound tightly together by a frame, making up a "form" or page. If done correctly, all letters were of the same height, and a flat surface of type was created. The form was placed in a press and inked and then printed (an impression made) on paper. Metal type read backwards, from right to left, and a key skill of the compositor was their ability to read this backwards text. The compositor machine was dubbed as "An Organ" and after just 15 minutes Tony was a "natural".

(The first edition of The Evening Post was printed by Thomas Forman on 1 May 1878. It sold for ½d and consisted of four pages.

In July 1963, the Nottingham Post's main competitor, the Nottingham Evening News, closed and merged with the Post. Also, the city's two morning papers, the Nottingham Daily Guardian and the Nottingham Journal, were merged into The Guardian Journal. On 19 June 1973, a printing dispute began, causing a period of industrial turmoil in the company, and The Guardian Journal ceased publication on that day. During the protracted dispute, some Post journalists launched their own newspaper, receiving moral support from Brian Clough, then manager of Nottingham Forest. Eventually, as the only remaining newspaper was the Nottingham Evening Post, which increasingly covered the whole day's news, it was re-named the Nottingham Post from the beginning of July 2010.

One of the Post's stalwart journalists, Emrys Bryson, wrote a revue about Nottingham life called "Owd Yer Tight", which ran at Nottingham's Theatre Royal. The Post's sister paper, the Nottinghamshire Weekly Guardian, published D. H. Lawrence's first short story, entitled "A Prelude", which won a prize in their December 1907 competition .

In March 1996 the Post was relaunched as a full-colour tabloid, although the Saturday edition had switched to the smaller paper size as far back as 1982.

The Post was based at offices on Forman Street in the centre of Nottingham until 1998 when then relocated to Castle Wharf House and moved again to Tollhouse Hill.)

On the day Britain declared war on Germany, 3 September 1939, Parliament immediately passed a more wide-reaching measure. The National Service (Armed Forces) Act imposed conscription on all males aged between 18 and 41 who had to register for service. Those medically unfit were exempted, as were others in key industries such as baking, farming, medicine and engineering.

Conscientious objectors, particularly Quakers had to appear before a tribunal to argue their reasons for refusing to join-up. If their cases were not dismissed, they were granted one of several categories of exemption and were given non-combatant jobs. Conscription helped greatly to increase the number of men in active service during the first year of the war.

Anthony, by then 19, was conscripted into a Nottinghamshire regiment and without any training was assigned as a private into the 2nd Battalion, Sherwood Foresters which was serving in the 3rd Infantry Brigade, part of the 1st Infantry Division, with which the battalion would remain with throughout the war. The division was sent to De Panne in Belgium, September 1939 shortly after the outbreak of the war, joining up with the British Expeditionary Force (BEF) in France seeing little action and put through limited basic training upon arrival. The battalion remained in France until May 1940 when the Germans invaded Luxembourg Belgium and Holland (The Low Countries). Then they took part in a short but bitter battle and were forced to be evacuated at Dunkirk as the BEF was in danger of being surrounded and overrun.

Having been shot in the buttocks Anthony was one of the unlucky thousands of the British Expeditionary Forces that were left in France after the evacuation of Dunkirk. They were expected to fight a rear-guard action, alongside of the French Army. This was in May/June 1940. Left behind was a hotch-potch of officers and senior NCOs from different regiments knowing nothing of what was going on. The untrained British troops were expected to fight a modern German Army with outdated weapons, much from the 1914-1918 War. Each squaddie was told not to do anything except to return rifle and machine gun fire when engaging the enemy.

Our soldiers were being wounded or killed but all that they could do was to fall back. They carried on the movement until reaching St Valery in France. It was here that they found other Units of the British Army and met up with the 51st Highland Division, which had been fighting a rear-guard action from the Maginot Line. With the 51st Highland Division and what remained of the other Units, they formed a great fighting force under the command of the French Army and on 12 June 1940, Then the French unexpectedly ordered the surrender of French and British troops to Field Marshall Rommel. German armies outflanked the intact Maginot Line and pushed deep into France, occupying Paris unopposed on 14 June. After the flight of the French government and the collapse of the French Army, German commanders met with French officials on 18 June to negotiate an end to hostilities. Italy entered the war on the German side on 10 June 1940 and attempted an invasion of France. On 22 June 1940, the Second Armistice at Compiègne was signed by France and Germany. The neutral Vichy government led by Marshal Philippe Pétain replaced the Third Republic and German military occupation began along the French North Sea and Atlantic coasts and their hinterlands.

The injured Anthony was transported across Belgium along with other British servicemen to a German Military Hospital just across the Dutch border. As a teenager Anthony was circumcised because of a continuous bacterial infection beneath his foreskin. In the German run hospital, he was anxious not to be thought to be a Jew. Fortunately, the medics that treated him were Dutch. When deemed well enough to travel, all injured POWs were herded in groups of 50 into train cattle carriages and transferred to Stalag VIIIB (Stalag 344) in Łambinowice (Lamsdor), Poland. Having skills useful to the Nazi regime Anthony was moved from Stalag VIIB to Stalag XXA in Toruń, before being located to a subcamp in Wyrzysk. It was there that he met and worked with British actor Sam Kydd, and they were allowed out to visit the local town. In the part they were billeted it was more of a collection of barracks with no watch towers or barbed wire fences.

Early in the Second World War, Sam Kydd went to France with the British Expeditionary Force but was quickly captured, spending the rest of the war in the subcamp.

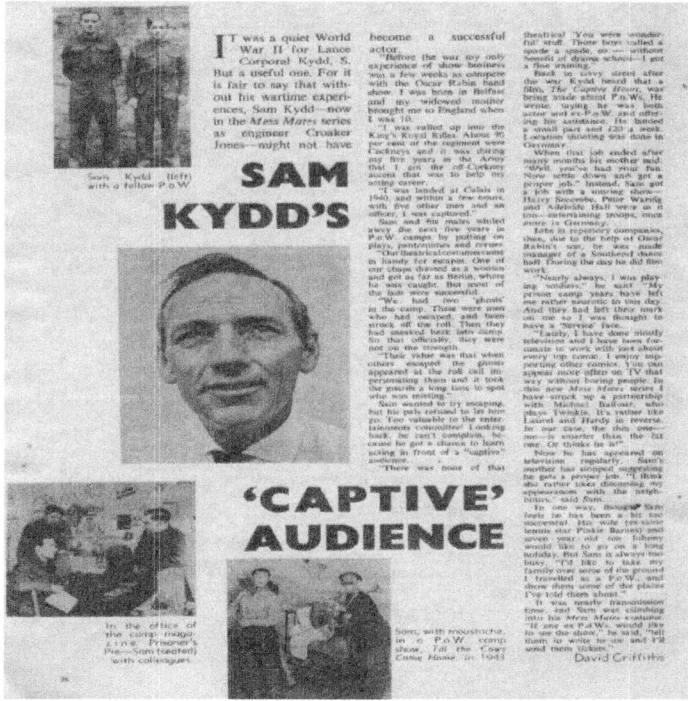

SAM KYDD'S 'CAPTIVE' AUDIENCE

By David Griffiths

Sam felt so strongly about his work there that, when he was offered repatriation after three years, Kydd turned it down to continue with his theatrical work. In recognition of his valuable services during these years he was awarded a pair of drama masks, made by the Red Cross from barbed wire.

Being what we would class today as an "open prison", Sam and Anthony learned various Polish phrases through contact with the local Polish population. Although Sam stayed behind, Anthony had other ideas and in 1941 disappeared and was "ghosted" so his German custodians were never aware that he was "absent without leave".

CHAPTER TWO

KEEP RIGHT ON TO THE END OF THE ROAD

In June 1941 Anthony went into the town of Wyrzysk and never returned to his POW billet. For the first couple of nights, he canoodled with his 15-year-old girlfriend Ada, the daughter of the local baker. She was a flighty young thing who had been seen "walking out" with German soldiers, so her affinity with the Boche enabled her to enjoy a protective aura by the occupiers, but a prevailing "Jerry Bag" reputation from the locals. Also, as daddy baked the bread and supplied black market delicacies from under-the-counter, her shield from actual aggression was ever present. For 48 hours Anthony was able to get a good feed in advance of his mighty trek to who knows where, and some sexual pleasures from Ada in the wheat store, next to the grinding machine – the miller not the young lady.

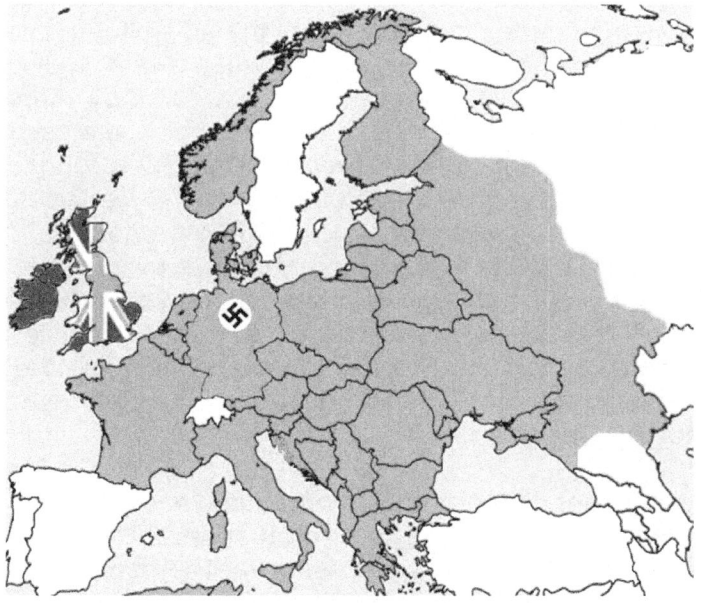

With most of Europe under the Nazi cosh his dilemma was whether he should walk north through Poland to a Baltic port and try a hitch a ride aboard a neutral Swedish freighter or southeast to Austria via Czechoslovakia to neutral Switzerland. As he assumed there might be many heavily fortified frontiers, then perhaps it would be better to go east into Germany (Anthony spoke fluent German) and then avoiding the low counties into Luxembourg then France and across the Pyrenees into neutral Spain. The walking distance from Wyrzysk to Luxembourg was a mere 2,550 miles.

Ada gave her British lover a handful of old maps which upon her dad's advice she had stolen from the schoolhouse just a few days before the German forces overran her town in 1939. In October and November 1939, as part of the Intelligenzaktion, the army supported by the German gendarmerie and Selbstschutz carried out mass arrests of local Poles, who then were imprisoned in the local court prison.

Many Poles from Wyrzysk, including teachers and priests, were among hundreds of Poles massacred by the Germans in the village of Paterek in October and November.

These maps were to prove to be invaluable to Anthony as he plotted a route into Germany to Potsdam – just south of Berlin. His journey of some 240 miles was to avoid main roads out of the town using farm tracks during the night heading to the agricultural township of Czarnków and during the day through what is now known as the Notecka Forest and the ancient Lubuska swampy marsh land, made up of 48% trees with the remainder being a mess of lakes and going nowhere tributaries. This is what our hiker found in 1941. The latter was grim and uninhabitable, but safe. He lived off fungi and nature-killed creatures and had to endure bouts of gastroenteritis. Unable to walk more than five miles a day his first 140 miles took until mid-August, but he was now only 30 miles from the German border. Not wanting to cross into Czechoslovakia he veered north east to Słubica a border town in the Lubusz Voivodeship, in western Poland. Located on the Oder river, which was a part of Dammvorstadt.

Now it was to get dangerous, but for an unexpected find of a dead German officer just inside of the Polish zone. "Like me he was a little bloke". Anthony swiftly devested the corpse of its uniform exchanging his tattered clothing for the full monty of a German officer. There were no identification papers on the Kraut who it appeared had either died of a stroke or heart attack, but his pockets

were stuffed with rolls of banded Reichsmarks almost 50,000 RM, at the time equivalent to a little over $30,000 US.
Would Oberleutnant Anthony pass muster when challenged by junior ranks requesting identification?

Stopping German Army transport heading for Berlin our Oberleutnant had to give it a try requesting that the driver diverted to Potsdam. The German Army had headquartered in Potsdam, during the year 1941, and it played a significant role in the military operations of Nazi Germany, and Anthony wanted to appear to be of immense importance. When dropped off outside the offices he quickly scurried away from the action.

Potsdam was a residence of the former Prussian kings and for the German Emperor Potsdam was intended as "a picturesque, pastoral dream" which would remind its residents of their relationship with nature. The city, which is over 1,000 years old, is widely known for its palaces, its lakes, and its overall historical and cultural significance. Landmarks include the parks and palaces of Sanssouci.

After the Nazis seized power in 1933, there was a ceremonial handshake, between President Paul von Hindenburg and the new Chancellor Adolf Hitler, in Potsdam's Garrison Church in what became known as the "Day of Potsdam". This symbolised a coalition of the military (Reichswehr) and Nazism.

Potsdam was also the location of the significant Potsdam Conference in 1945, the conference where the three heads of government of the USSR (Stalin), the US(Truman), and the UK

(Churchill) decided on the division of Germany following its surrender, a conference which would define Germany's history for the next 45 years. Interestingly Babelsberg, in the south-eastern part of Potsdam, was since the 1930s the home of a major film production studio, The Babelsberg Film Studio, founded in 1912, is thought to be the oldest large-scale film studio in the world.

A couple of nights in the best hotel in town which wasn't really at hotel - the Potsdam City Palace had become the   HQ for SS Officers and high-ranking military personnel.

CHAPTER THREE: SHOUT LIKE A KRAUT

Anthony realised that although he wore the trappings of a German Army Officer, he needed some form of identification. Adopting a belligerent attitude and bellowing like an angry bull intimidated lesser ranks who asked to see his paperwork, but such behaviour could only be a one-time performance. His acting skills, being honed to perfection because of his association with British actor Sam Kydd in the POW subcamp in Poland were now being tested. After a couple of nights at the City Palace in Potsdam it was time to move on.

Taking a train was the answer. When in 1920 the national German train company was founded it was known as the Deutsche Reichseisenbahnen ("German Imperial Rail") when the Weimar Republic, which still used the nation-state term of the previous monarchy, Deutsches Reich (German Reich, hence the usage of the word "Reich" in the logo name of the railway. With some deference to the Keiser the term was Deutsches Kaiserreich), took national control of the German railways, which had previously been run by the German states (<u>Länderbahnen</u>). Five years later it was renamed   the "German Imperial Railway Company", DRG, a nominally private railway company, which was 100% owned by the German state. In 1937 the railway was reorganised again by the government state authority and given the name "Deutsche Reichsbahn" (German Imperial Railway, DRB). After the Anschluss in 1938 the DR also took over the Bundesbahn Österreich ("Federal Railway of Austria", BBÖ). Now under the control of the Nazi regime its prime tasks were military transportation into the occupied countries, and the barbaric movement of Jews to a variety of concentration camps. There was a regular ordinary passenger train service to Leipzig and a uniformed officer buying a ticket did not require any identification.

On 9 November 1938, as part of Kristallnacht, in Leipzig on Gottschedstrasse, synagogues and businesses were set on fire. Only a couple of days later, on 11 November 1938, many Jews in the Leipzig area were deported to the Buchenwald Concentration Camp. During the German invasion of Poland at the start of World War II, in September 1939, the Gestapo carried out arrests of prominent local Poles, and seized the Leipzig Polish Consulate and its library. In 1941, the American Consulate was also closed by order of the German authorities. During the war, Leipzig was the location of five subcamps of the Buchenwald concentration camp, in which over 8,000 men, women and children were imprisoned,

mostly Polish, Jewish, British, Belgian and French. So, for Anthony it was a city in turmoil, but it also had an Anti-Nazi commune. Hopefully these guys could counterfeit a bunch of authentic looking documents. His first port of call was a tailor to buy some civilian clothing, because he could hardly rock up dressed as a German Officer trying to locate the "underground."

Elfriede Remark (pictured left) grew up in Osnabrück. Her brother was Erich Maria Remarque, the author of the well-known anti-war novel All Quiet on the Western Front. After training as a dressmaker, she ran her own salon in Leipzig. In 1941 she married Erich Scholz. Elfriede Scholz made no secret of her critical stance toward National Socialism and war. She told an acquaintance and customer at her tailoring shop that she did not believe in the propaganda of a German "final victory" and that the German soldiers on the front were nothing but "beasts for the slaughter." She also said she would kill Adolf Hitler. This lady was the key to his problems, but how could Tony visit her shop dressed as the enemy? Getting a billet for the night in the local German Officers Club, he disappeared into the night to steal any clothing he could find. There was nothing hanging on any washing line, but there were cast off clothes in the bins at the back of a local funeral director's salon. As older people shrink with age there was no difficulty in finding anything to fit his 5'4" frame.

He left the officers' club the following morning dressed in his collection of cast-off muftis and relocated in an anonymous pension. Having spent little of the 50,000 Reichsmarks he found stuffed in the pockets of the dead German officer he unearthed in Słubica, Poland, he was a very wealthy young man.

Finding Elfriede's dress making and tailoring establishment he ordered a new business suit, shirts, a tie and underpants, the latter being a welcome addition to his wardrobe having been travelling "commando" for months. The proprietress said she couldn't do it as she couldn't stock any cloth – a generous 1,000RM bribe and the deal was done. Now it was time for the great confessional for Anthony to admit that he was an escapee Brit travelling in sheep's clothing and needing forged German Military ID. Elfriede vomited, terrified that she was about to be arrested in what could be a Gestapo sting.

"I have no ID; I am an ordinary English soldier trying to get back to England. Tie me up and get your people to interrogate me. I am the vulnerable one here Elfriede. I am the one at risk. If your people do not believe me, I know I will be killed. I have more than enough money to survive, so you ou can have some of it to help your cause. I can tell you what I have seen in Poland – I can help you – I prostrate myself into your capture, so please believe me."

In October the over-night temperature averaged 6°C (43°F) and Anthony was to be bound and gagged for three days in a storeroom, before his anti-Nazi interrogators arrived. His belongings were gathered up from his B & B including his officer's uniform – the latter at least confirming part of his story.

Then three masked German guys arrived together with Sally, an un-masked English lady who he guessed might be a spy working with the resistance and did their dastardly deeds to confirm his stories. But what resistance would there be in the Fatherland unless it related to RAF aircrew who avoided being killed when their 'planes were shot down? If this was the case, then he might be a candidate for a place in a Lysander. The Westland Lysander was a British army co-operation and a liaison type of aircraft produced by Westland Aircraft Corp. that was used immediately before and during the Second World War. (Picture below shows a Westland Lysander Mk.III (SD) in overall black camouflage as used for special night missions during World War II.)

The high-lift devices gave the Lysander a short take-off and landing performance much appreciated by the Special Duties pilots. The wings were equipped with automatic slats which lifted away from the leading edge as the airspeed decreased towards stalling speed. These slats controlled automatic flaps. Slow speed flight was therefore greatly simplified. The inboard slats were connected to the flaps and to an air damper in the port wing which governed the speed at which the slats operated. The outboard slats operated independently and were not connected, and each was fitted with an air damper. On a normal approach, the inboard slats and the flaps would begin to open when the airspeed has dropped to about 85 mph and be approximately half down at 80 mph. The only control that the pilot has is a locking lever which he can set to lock the flaps down once they have been lowered automatically. Well, that is the technical bit, the difficult aspect was the range which was around 600 miles meaning the craft would have to be manually refuelled when landed for the return journey.

It had been done once before from the east of Germany and although there was only capacity for one pilot and one passenger a second injured airman was stretchered into the Lysander and strapped to the floor.

On this occasion it was to up for consideration to ferry Anthony back to their home-based airfield in Newmarket, Suffolk but as he was a mere soldier, and a lowly private at that, and airmen took priority. Radio operator Sally was however able to transmit b to Whitehall with his name, rank, number, and regiment details to confirm his identity and his mum was contacted to let her know that a previous "missing in action – presumed dead" message was rescinded and replaced with better news. Sally and her team did arrange for an overnight production of German officer passes like the illustration below:

And together with a train ticket to Koblenz for "Oberleutnant Anton Heidelberg" – Anton being the German equivalent to Anthony (actor Anton Diffring, who incidentally being Jewish and a homosexual left Germany for Britain prior to WWII to avoid internment and worked as an interpreter for the War Office before becoming a film star always cast as a Nazi Officer) and Heidelberg the brand of one of the printing machines he operated at the Nottingham Evening Post.

CHAPTER FOUR: CHEERS or PROST, GERSUNDHEIT or ZUM WOHL

Koblenz is a German city on the banks of the Rhine and the Moselle, and as such benefitted greatly by being a multinational community. It ranks in population behind Mainz and Ludwigshafen am Rhein to be the third-largest city in Rhineland-Palatinate. In 1942 there were some 100,000 inhabitants excluding military personnel, with many working in the wine growing and bottling industry. Koblenz lies in a narrow flood plain between high hill ranges, some reaching mountainous height, and it is part of the populous Rhineland. As well as grapes the mild climate allows fig trees, olive trees, palm trees and other mediterranean plants to grow in the area.

Anchored out of Koblenz the first Army Group B was created on 12 October 1939 (from the former Army Group North) and fought in the Battle of France on the northern flank. It was responsible for a part of the German invasion of Belgium and Holland. During the majority of the later stage of that campaign ("Case Red"), it again advanced on the German right flank towards the Somme river, the city of Paris and the Franco-Spanish border.

After 16 August 1940, it was deployed to East Prussia and to the Government in German-occupied Poland. When Operation Barbarossa began on 22 June 1941, Army Group B was renamed on the same day to become "Army Group Centre".

(On 26 November 1943, another Army Group B command was created at the coast of the English Channel in German-occupied France. After the Allied Normandy landings in June 1944, Army Group B initially commanded the northern wing of the new Western Front. It is notable on the Western Front as the army group to oversee the German Ardennes Offensive ("Battle of the Bulge"). Eventually, Army Group B surrendered on 17 April 1945 in the Ruhr pocket.)

So, what is Anthony doing in Koblenz? It was a staging point on his journey but there was nothing to do. It was here that his "Anton Heidelberg" ID was put to the test. A cursory glance and he was through to the officers' accommodation section of the Army Forces Command (German: Heeresführungskommando) in Falckenstein Barracks in Koblenz was one of the two leadership pillars of the German Army, together with the German Army Office, before it was merged into the Army Command (Kommando Heer).

It was now winter, and Koblenz was not where Anthony wanted to be. Having to make small talk to drunken German officers draped over by semi naked prostitutes imported from Poland was an anathema to his every senses. He longed for the comfort of his Polish Ada. He didn't want to fornicate with the imported tarts, though as his abstention might be suspect, he went to his room and left early the following morning to avoid being confronted with any other offensive debauchery. Military transport was on offer to the Grand Duchy of Luxembourg. Some members of their Royal Family had been "sacredly" removed to London under the guise of being members of the local Catholic representatives of the Vatican. To the average European the country of Luxembourg means Radio Luxembourg, and the English Language service in particular which began broadcasting light entertainment shows to the UK 90 years ago. Sponsors included Halls therapeutic wine, Zam-Buk a cure-all ointment for pain, burns, cuts and bruises, Do-Do a linctus for asthma sufferers, Littlewoods and Vernons Football Pools, and the League of Ovaltineys. In the years from 1933 to 1939, the English-language service of Radio Luxembourg gained a large audience in the UK and other European countries, with sponsored programming aired from noon until midnight on Sundays and at various times during the rest of the week. Around 11% of Britons listened to it during the week, preferring Luxembourg's light music and variety programmes to the BBC. Up to half of Britons did so before 10:15 am on weekdays when the BBC did not broadcast, and at weekends when it followed the "Lord Reith Sunday" schedule of only serious and religious programmes. Reith was the fifth son and the youngest, by ten years, of the seven children of the Rev. George Reith, a Scottish Presbyterian minister of the College Church at Glasgow and later Moderator of the United Church of Scotland. He was to carry strict Presbyterian religious convictions forward into his adult life, influencing his puritanical grip of the BBC airwaves when he became controller. In the late 1950s the English service of Radio Luxembourg was the pop station for all of Europe. Cliff Richard even when his records were played on the station admitted that he never realised that Luxembourg was a country, and whilst stationed in the US Army in Germany Elvis Presley chose to listen to 208 in preference to the American Forces Network, and as well as receiving the first European plays of all his discs as too did the Beatles.

A group of holiday-making English Radio Luxembourg fans, pictured in front of the main entrance to the Villa Louvigny broadcast studios . The date is Wednesday 9 August 1939, three weeks before the declaration of war.

On 21 September 1939, the Luxembourg government closed the radio station in an abortive attempt to protect its neutrality. The station and powerful transmitters were taken over by the invading German forces in 1940 from which they would use to air propaganda broadcasts all over Europe and beyond.

The most famous English language propaganda voice was that of William Joyce, aka Lord Haw Haw. For the first years of WW2 his broadcasts came from Berlin, but severe bombing of the German capital meant that he had to relocate to Luxembourg.

On 21 September 1939, the Luxembourg government closed the radio station in an abortive attempt to protect its neutrality. The station and powerful transmitters were taken over by the invading German forces in 1940 from which they would use to air propaganda broadcasts all over Europe and beyond.
The most famous English language propaganda voice was that of William Joyce, aka Lord Haw Haw. For the first years of WW2 his broadcasts came from Berlin, but severe bombing of the German capital meant that he had to relocate to Luxembourg.

CHAPTER FIVE: THE GRAND DUCHESS OF LUXEMBOURG

During World War II our BBC played a crucial role in allowing exiled, the Grand Duchess Charlotte, to speak to Luxembourg population. On 5 September 1940, the voice of Grand Duchess Charlotte of Luxembourg to broadcast over the BBC's airwaves, for the first time, and in her speech she appealed to the country not to give up hope, saying that by going into exile she was able to appeal to the allies to fight for the freedom of the country. Foreign Minister Joseph Besch, also in exile with the government in London, arranged with the BBC to have a regular Luxembourg programme. Under an agreement with the foreign office, there was just a five-minute programme at 8pm on the last day of the month, for months with 30 days, and a 15-minute programme on the last day of every month. On 29 December 1940, the Luxembourg national anthem was broadcast by the BBC for the first time.

By March 1941 a new deal with the BBC was struck, for a new Luxembourg programme scheduled from 8am to 8.15am every Sunday. Léon Clasen, son of Luxembourg's honorary consul to London, was placed in charge of managing the broadcast. From March 1943 Luxembourg was then expanded to four weekly broadcasts lasting 15 minutes. Starting October 1943, the London to Luxembourg programme aired daily, with special segments dedicated to important events such as the general strike in September 1942 or the silver throne jubilee of the Grand Duchess in 1944. Luxembourgers were updated on political events, but also the lives of the Grand Ducal family in exile. Charlotte herself frequently contributed to these programmes.

Oberleutnant Anton Heidelberg having boarded a troop train in Leipzig arrived in the early evening towards the end of May 1943 at Bahnhof Luxemburg. Next to the train station was the luxurious Alfa Hotel. It was taken over by a few German officers. The Gestapo were in the Villa Pauly mansion a mile away from the Alfa, housed in rooms out of earshot of their prisoners who were manacled within the torture chambers. From August 1940 to September 1944, this building was the exclusive headquarters of the Geheime Staatspolizei in Luxembourg and the symbol of the oppression. In the basement, people were questioned and tortured. (Today the building houses a documentation centre about the resistance movement.)

Anthony decided that with sufficient money to live well above his station, in this splendid hotel and having yomped across Eastern Europe, he needed a few months respite. Resplendent in his German officer's uniform the kowtowing of the staff in reception and the dining room gave "Anton" an uncomfortable feeling of their exaggerated deference. He so wanted to tell them that he was "on their side" but common sense prevailed.

The Belgian and Luxembourg men and women working at the Alfa were in their 60s, though the young 20-year-old scantily dressed "barfly" ladies were provided and funded by the Wehrmacht. One could say as they were harvested from all the occupied territories "Prostituierte ohne Grenzen". In amongst the bevy of beauties "Anton" was surprised to see African ladies in attendance. Black Germans experienced discrimination in employment, welfare, and housing, and were also banned from pursuing higher education; they were socially isolated and forbidden to have sexual relations and marriages with Aryans by the racial law. Within the confines of the Alfa they were they were "trophy conquests" by some Army

Officers, but these clandestine courtships had to be concealed from the prying eyes of the Gestapo.

The food was well prepared, and the meat was almost always wild boar or deer procured for the kitchens by local poachers. Wine was in abundance, but the bread was always hard and brown. The central focus of Germany's war policy for food was achieved by conquering Poland and the fertile chernozem, or "black earth," region of Ukraine and neighbouring republics of the Soviet Union, by expelling, starving or killing the native populations. German farmers were to be resettled on the vacated lands, thus assuring Germany self-sufficiency in food and enabling Germany to take a secure place alongside the United Kingdom and the United States as a world power. As it worked out, Poland and Ukraine became only minor contributors of food to the civilian population of Germany, as more food came from western European countries such as France and Denmark. To maintain domestic agricultural production while millions of men were serving in the military, Germany imported millions of women and men workers from forced labour, and concentration camps. A starving Jew seen trying to eat a carrot whilst picking the crop for his master was shot on the spot.

The activities of the resistance in Luxembourg were largely directed towards undermining the German monopoly on information, and providing moral support to the population, by spreading counterpropaganda by word-of-mouth, leaflets, posters, and later whole newspaper. It was here that with an anti-Nazi Belgian waiter, who he had befriended, Anthony helped with the printing using dilapidated equipment. Paper was the most difficult commodity to find, but the Church had quantities in abundance. The Catholic Church in Luxembourg was relatively silent during the war, and took no public stance regarding the fate of the Jews or the Nazi regime. On the one hand, the Bishop, Joseph Laurent Philippe, was bedridden, and was therefore in no state to provide active opposition, but he did agree to meet with fellow Catholic Anthony and subsequently relinquished his paper stock. On the other hand, the bishop did not want to further antagonise the occupiers and endanger the already precarious religious life of the Church, which was heavily restricted during wartime. Bishop Philippe had refused to meet with the local Nazi leadership.

Additionally, the resistance helped Allied POWs, shot-down pilots, "deserters" from the Wehrmacht, Jews and other endangered Luxembourgers to cross the borders into Belgium or France.

The introduction of forced labour and conscription into the Wehrmacht added to the Resistance's tasks: many youths who refused to serve in the German armed forces now had to be hidden around the country and kept safe and fed or helped to escape abroad. Collections of food and money were also made to help the families of those who were arrested, deported, or fired from their jobs. An increasingly important part of the resistance's activities was to provide military, political and economic intelligence to the Allies.

Despite its small size and neutrality, Luxembourg played a significant role in WWII, both as a victim of occupation and as a key player in the resistance to the German occupation. Anthony was seconded to become their anti-Nazi propaganda printer, yet it didn't come without risks. When leaving the Alfa, he though it wise to dress as in his officers' uniform surrounding himself with those of similar ranks. Only then was it safe and easy then to slip down a side street and visit the mortician's parlour whose cellar not only hosted the deceased but housed the printing equipment.

The English Service of Radio Luxembourg 1933 – 1939

On 1 January 1933 Stephen Williams, Directeur-Général of Radio-Publicity, a British company chaired by Frenchman Jacques Gonat, which operated the concession for English programmes at Radio Paris, began presenting sponsored broadcasts from the French capital. Because commercial broadcasting was prohibited at the time in the UK, sponsored programmes in English were broadcast from the continent (Radio Normandy, Radio Lyons, Radio Toulouse, Poste Parisien, Radio Paris). As Radio Paris was to become a state-run national station, an alternative had to be found for broadcasting English programmes. What better alternative than the most modern and powerful transmitter in Europe? On Sunday 3 December, English programmes are simultaneously broadcast from Radio Paris and Radio Luxembourg and finally transferred permanently to Luxembourg the following Sunday. The international and multilingual programming of Radio Luxembourg was a huge success in Germany, Great Britain, France, and Belgium, and astonished CLR's competitors. Concerns were raised especially by the BBC and the British Post Office concerning the power of the transmitter that enabled Radio Luxembourg to be broadcast throughout Britain, undermining the BBC's monopoly. The British authorities also protested vehemently against the wavelength (1250 metres) chosen by the Radio Luxembourg management, and which has been denied to the Grand Duchy at the European Broadcasting Conference in Lucerne, claiming it would interfere with British aircraft wireless services. The BBC tried to persuade leading British newspapers not to publish the Radio Luxembourg schedules. 1934: In February, Radio Luxembourg switched to a new wavelength of 1304 metres, which had been allocated to Warsaw by the Lucerne Wavelength Plan. This is regarded as illegal by the International Broadcasting Union who had however no coercive power. English programmes from Luxembourg enjoyed growing popularity among British listeners, especially as the Sunday broadcasts on the BBC are rather austere in accordance with the Sunday Observance restrictions, whereas Radio Luxembourg broadcast jazz and light music.

Christopher Stone joined the commercial station Radio Luxembourg in September. This sensational move was considered an act of lèse-majesté by the prim BBC, who consequently blacklists him as well as other British artists who worked with Radio Luxembourg. 1936: A legal battle between the CLR and Radio Publicity (London), the English language concession company, lead to the revocation of the concession in favour of the newly created Wireless Publicity Ltd, which was a subsidiary of the ostensibly private firm Cable & Wireless Ltd, whose vast undersea cable network was the subject of considerable British government interest and secret subsidies. Under the impulse of this new agent, Radio Luxembourg expanded with daily programmes in English. 1937: Following the ongoing success of Radio Luxembourg, CLR bought the Villa Louvigny and extended the premises. 1938: From May 1938 to September 1939 a De Havilland Dragon airplane christened 'The Luxembourg Listener' (Olley Air Service) commenced a twice weekly return trip from Croydon to Esch-sur-Alzette carrying taped programmes, records, and passengers. In Britain audience figures peaked at around four million.

Under the impulse of this new agent, Radio Luxembourg expanded with daily programmes in English. 1937: Following the ongoing success of Radio Luxembourg, CLR bought the Villa Louvigny and extended the premises. 1938: From May 1938 to September 1939 a De Havilland Dragon airplane christened 'The Luxembourg Listener' (Olley Air Service) commenced a twice weekly return trip from Croydon to Esch-sur-Alzette carrying taped programmes, records, and passengers. In Britain audience figures peaked at around four million.

Presenters: Christopher Stone and Stephen Williams in the studio at Villa Louvigny in Luxembourg City.

Christopher Stone joined the English Service in 1934 and was paid a staggering £5,000 a year which is today almost equivalent to half a million quid. Upon his return to London, he was barred by the BBC but such was his popularity he returned to the Light Programme in 1940. On 11 November 1941 he wished King Victor Emmanuel of Italy a happy birthday on air, adding "I don't think any of us wish him anything but good, poor soul." This good wish towards the head of a state with which Britain was at war at the time led to the sacking of the BBC's Senior Controller of Programmes and tighter government control over all broadcasts. Stone was an avid record collector; in the mid-1930s he already owned over 12,000. When he turned 75 in 1957 the magazine Melody Maker praised his pioneering work: "Everyone who has written, produced or compered a gramophone programme should salute the founder of his trade."

Stephen Williams was literally the first Pirate Radio DJ. During his university vacation in 1928 he got a job as announcer on a "broadcasting yacht" sponsored by the Daily Mail newspaper group. This vessel went round the coast of Britain, transmitting music on records and advertisements for the Daily Mail, from just outside territorial waters, an early precursor of the 1960s "pirate radio" ships. After a stint with Radio Paris and Radio Normandy in December 1933, Williams became the first English radio presenter in Luxembourg as well as serving as manager of the station. Returning to Luxembourg after the ward Stephen Williams resumed his duties. He left Luxembourg in 1948 and worked until 1975 as a freelance broadcaster.

Footnote: (When, on 1 January 1992, Radio Luxembourg's English service closed as a terrestrial radio station, the last words heard, "Good luck, good listening ... and goodbye" were spoken by 83-year-old Stephen Williams, who had been the first person ever to say on the air "This is Radio Luxembourg" over 58 years earlier. That day he was awarded the Order of Merit of the Grand Duchy of Luxembourg by the Grand Duke of Luxembourg.) 1939: On the eve of war, the Luxembourg government, concerned about maintaining Luxembourg's neutrality, asks CLR to stop broadcasting – a decision already considered by the company's management. Regular programmes cease on 2 September, and broadcasting is limited to official government communiques and music. Less than three weeks later, operations are closed.

CHAPTER SIX: GERMANY CALLING

Radio was still a relatively new technology at the time the Nazi Party rose to power in 1933. The first regular radio broadcasts in

Germany began only a decade earlier during the years of the Weimar Republic. Radio receivers were luxury items when they were first introduced, and only a small percentage of Germans had them in their homes. But home radio ownership was growing by the time that the Nazi Party rose to power

Radio became the leading form of mass communication during that time, When Adolf Hitler was appointed German Chancellor the Nazi regime immediately began consolidating its power and reshaping German society in a process known as coordination "Gleichschaltung" . Nazi leaders saw the control of Germany's radio broadcasting networks as a crucial part of these efforts to transform Germany. The regime used radio to spread Nazi propaganda and create a sense of shared culture and community among members of the Nazis' so-called "national community" ("Volksgemeinschaft").

Joseph Goebbels understood the art of persuasion. As propaganda minister for the Nazis, he sought to exploit radio's tremendous potential to broadcast Hitler's messages. But first he needed a way for people to tune in. "Radio helped bring the Nazis to power and keep them there," he said, so on 18 August 1933, Goebbels opened the 10th International Radio Show, in Berlin, with a speech declaring "Radio as the Eighth Great Power" a nod to Napoleon's notion that the press was the seventh great power. Goebbels argued that "the radio will be for the twentieth century what the press was for the nineteenth century." He noted the failure of the Weimar Republic to embrace radio and claimed that the National Socialists would not have been able to take power without it. Advertisements positioned the Volksempfänger as the intermediary for the greater German community that would make the country strong and prosperous again by bringing political, cultural, and economic ideas into every household. The national emblem of the eagle near the tuning dial identifies the product as part of state propaganda efforts. Later models also included a swastika.

An even cheaper version of the radio, the Kleinemfänger (illustrated above) came out in 1938 and sold for 35 Reichsmarks. It earned the nickname Goebbels-Shnauze, or "Goebbels' snout," partly because it looked like a big blunt nose, but mostly because it was the mouthpiece for Goebbel. "We want a radio that reaches the people, a radio that works for the people, a radio that is an intermediary between the government and the nation, a radio that also reaches across our borders to give the world a picture of our character, our life, and our work," Goebbels proclaimed. To make that happen, Geobbels had seized total control over the Gesellschaft, the Reich Broadcasting Corporation, a national network of regional broadcasting companies. After solidifying control of the broadcast infrastructure, he imposed rules on permissible content. His final task was to make sure everyone had access to an affordable radio receiver. But radios in Germany in the early 1930s were expensive, easily exceeding a month's wages for ordinary workers. Nazi leaders thought radio could be used to connect and unite the active members of their community especially during World War II. The variety of different programming including anti-Jewish propaganda, news about the war and music was part of the mind shaping roll of broadcast radio in Germany. Popular Sunday programming in Nazi Germany featured songs that were requested for loved ones serving on the front as well as personal announcements such as births or engagements. These personal details were included to produce emotional responses in listeners. Propagandists hoped to create the feeling that the members of their " Nazi national community" all belonged to one gigantic, extended national family united by a stream of words and music.

The regime also tried using radio to connect civilians with the experiences of those serving in the German military by broadcasting news and propaganda from the front, using the voices of members of the German military reporting from the frontlines as battle scenes play behind them. "Listening to the radio could connect loved ones separated by war through shared experiences. Nazi leaders imagined that radio would act like a "magical bond" uniting Germans on the home front with soldiers on the frontlines.

To increase the size of the listening audience for Nazi radio broadcasts, the regime started production of the so-called "People's Receiver" ("Volksempfänger") in May 1933. These basic and affordable radio sets enabled the regime to broadcast Nazi propaganda directly into listeners' homes. They were intended to show that the Nazi regime was improving Germans' quality of life and erasing class differences among members of the national community, "People's Receivers" were designed to pick up local German stations only, but listeners could sometimes pick up foreign broadcasts. Listening to foreign radio broadcasts became a punishable offense after the outbreak of World War II. Many Germans risked tuning in anyway, but if discovered punishments included fines, property and home confiscations, imprisonment and even execution.   During World War II, Nazi authorities began registering the names and addresses of anyone who bought new radios and confiscated radios owned by Jews.

In the British Isles there were no prohibitions for people wanting to tune into foreign even propagandistic broadcasts, and initially the Fleet Street newspapers listed the broadcast frequences. In all the occupied countries across Europe, radio sets were confiscated by Germans, and those found to be listening to the BBC were shot.

Most effective among the Nazis broadcasting to the UK was William Joyce. This Irish-American fascist, known in Britain as "Lord Haw-Haw", won a large audience during the "phoney war" in 1939 and early 1940, with his trademark call sign delivered in his unmistakable accent: "Jairmany calling, Jairmany calling".

Olivia Cockett, a diarist for the Mass Observation project that recorded the everyday thoughts of British people of the period, illustrated the popularity of such broadcasts. Her diary entry for 13 October 1939 records that she "took tea up to my sitting room to listen to the German news in English. They sound mostly quite as reasonable and convincing as the BBC so that I am more than ever wondering where the truth lies". The idea that Haw-Haw was a privileged member of the upper classes also gained widespread currency, and reinforced the belief that he might have access to important information. The myth of the English aristocrat with inside knowledge of the German high command was all powerful.

It inspired controversy within the pages of The Times. On 2 January 1940, a letter disputed the suggestion that Haw-Haw sounded upper class. Acknowledged that he "speaks excellent English", the writer did not believe it to be "public school" English. The newspaper then invited other readers to share their opinions. Six days later the Times collated their responses in a news story. One reader was perceptively certain that Haw-Haw's speech indicated that he had Irish origins. Another detected "the pomposity and condescension associated with privilege and class". The headmaster of King Edward VI School in Nuneaton added: "His broadcasts are a joy, and he has added to the gaiety of nations."

This capacity to entertain alarmed the popular, left-of-centre Daily Mirror. It suggested that the BBC should rebut Haw-Haw's assertions. If it was true that innocent folk listening to Haw-Haw have indeed begun to fall under the spell of his prestige perhaps some equally bland announcer should answer him back every evening and refute the most perilous part of his propaganda, which is probably his not unskilful appeal to socialist and anti-imperialist suspicions. The conservative Daily Mail was equally aware that its readers enjoyed Haw-Haw. It deprecated his "vicious little wisecracks" and deplored his "insinuating questions".

In the BBC's own magazine, The Listener, in January 1940, a reader expressed his fear that consistent bombardment by such propaganda might lead British listeners to question the accuracy of the BBC's own reporting. He feared that "the only solution will be to emulate Germany's example and make it an offence to listen to foreign broadcasting". As tempting though it was, a ban on listening would make a mockery of Britain's commitment to democratic principles. American opinion would be outraged. The solution was not censorship but a determined effort to raise the entertainment value of BBC radio. Lord Haw-Haw played a part in shifting the BBC away from its policy of ignoring popular preferences to an understanding that "the barometer of listeners' preferences" should help to define its output.

Great wartime BBC radio shows were devised that attracted colossal audiences and made the image of a family gathered around a radio set genuinely representative of wartime Britain. Soon, radio overtook newspapers as Britain's primary source of news and entertainment, with John Snagg reading it. (below)

"Music While You Work", "Housewives Choice", and the star-studded "It's That Man Again" (commonly contracted to ITMA) was a BBC radio comedy programme which ran for twelve series from 1939 throughout the war and for four years thereafter. The shows featured Tommy Handley in the central role, a fast-talking figure, around whom the other characters orbited. The programmes were written by Ted Kavanagh and produced by Francis Worsley. ITMA was a fast-delivered caustic character-driven comedy whose satirical targets included officialdom and the proliferation of minor wartime regulations. Parts of the scripts were rewritten in the hour before the broadcast, to ensure breaking news and topicality. ITMA broke away from the conventions of previous radio comedies, and from the humour of the music halls. The shows used sound effects in a novel manner, which, alongside a wide range of voices and accents, created the programme's atmosphere.

The show presented more than seventy regular characters during its twelve seasons, most of them with his or her own catchphrase.

Among them were the bibulous Colonel Chinstrap ("I don't mind if I do"), the charlady Mrs Mopp ("Can I do you now, sir?"), the incompetent German agent Funf ("this is Funf speaking"), the courtly odd-job men Cecil and Claude ("After you, Claude, no, after you, Cecil"), the Middle Eastern hawker Ali Oop ("I go and I come back"), and the lugubrious Mona Lott ("It's being so cheerful that keeps me going"). The programmes on tour cast pictured below.

Workers' Playtime was a British radio variety programme transmitted by the BBC from 1941· Originally intended as a morale-booster for industrial workers in Britain during World War II, the programme was broadcast at lunchtime, three times a week, live from a factory canteen "somewhere in Britain". Initially, it was broadcast simultaneously on both networks: the BBC Home Service and Forces Programme.. Each show concluded with the words from the show's producer, Bill Gates: "Good luck, all workers!"

Many famous variety, vocal and comedy artists appeared over the years, such as Charlie Chester, Arthur Askey, Bob and Alf Pearson, Bob Monkhouse, Peter Sellers, Tony Hancock, Frankie Howerd, Terry-Thomas, Anne Shelton, Betty Driver (Betty Turpin in

Coronation Street) , Eve Boswell, Vera Lynn (above), Arthur English (above), and Gert and Daisy (Elsie and Doris Waters) and many more.

The programme had the support of the government because the shows were seen as supporting the war effort on the home front. Workers' Playtime was a touring show, with the Ministry of Labour choosing which factory canteens it would visit.

THREE MONTHS AGO HE WAS AN ALDERSHOT PAINTER : Arthur English, now appearing in his third Windmill show

Throughout World War II, Ernest Bevin, the Minister of Labour and National Service, would appear on these shows from time to time to congratulate the workers and exhort them to greater efforts. When the war ended it was realised that the show had worked, which meant that Ernest Bevin wanted Workers' Playtime to continue to raise the morale of the workers, whilst the government rebuilt Britain and the British economy. The BBC, for its part, was very happy to continue with a show which had proved a national success even if it did mean transporting crew, cable, microphones, two pianos, a producer, two pianists and a group of variety artists up and down the country three times a week.

On 15 October 1940 a delayed action 225kg bomb smashed through a seventh-floor window of the BBC's Broadcasting House, before coming to rest in the music library two floors below. It exploded just after 9.00pm, when attempts were made to move it, killing 4 men and 3 women.

Meanwhile, back in Luxembourg, two medics, Jānis and Agnese Semjonova, were pressed into service, shortly following the military occupation of Latvia on 10 July 1941, by Germany's armed forces. Initially, the territory of Latvia was under the military administration of German Army Group North, but on 25 July 1941, Latvia was incorporated as Generalbezirk Lettland, and subsequently subordinated to Reichskommissariat Ostland, an administrative subdivision. Agnese was a hospital doctor and Jānis, a leading chiropractor. They were moved from Riga to Luxembourg and given an apartment with a connecting door with access to a smaller bedroom which was to be their treatment centre.

The raucous behaviour of the German Officers was a mixture of lewd debauchery and paralytic drunkenness. Sexual activities with the imported Polish girls were often in full view of others, and our Oberleutnant Anton Heidelberg became tempted to be involved in the affray, but never dared to display his cut genitalia in public. Doctor Agnese Semjonova, the attractive wife of Jānis, could not avoid the perverse advances of the young officers and concluded with her husband that it was better to join in than be ostracised. Jānis encouraged his wife to enjoy her nocturnal flings because he had his own agenda entertaining a couple of the bi-sexual German Officers.

Caught up in the maelstrom of bodies booze and vomit Anton slipped awkwardly falling on his hip. He was in agony, stretchered out to Jānis' treatment room.

Our chiropractor had healing hands and a slow but forceful massage helped to release the knots and sooth his battered body parts. Over the next few days there were many visits to the Alfa Hotel's treatment room, which explained why Jānis encouraged his beautiful wife to sleep around., but Anton did not succumb to his advances. At the end of the treatment Anton was invited to spend the night with the lady Doctor. As for his circumcision the Latvian swingers never mentioned it. It was apparent that both medics were very much anti-Nazi but in this caustic environment each must play his or her part to ensure survival.

As well as sex and booze drugs were also freely available throughout the German military, particularly in a society hell bent on keeping up with the energetic Hitler ("Germany awake!" the Nazis ordered, and the nation had no choice but to snap to attention). A substance that could "integrate shirkers, malingerers, defeatists and whiners" into the labour market was administered. Within the Temmler pharmaceutical company in Berlin, head chemist Dr Fritz Hauschild, inspired by the successful use of the American amphetamine Benzedrine at the 1936 Olympic Games, began trying to develop his own wonder drug – and a year later, he patented the first German methyl-amphetamine.

Pervitin, as it was known, quickly became a sensation, used as a confidence booster and performance enhancer by everyone from secretaries to actors to train drivers (initially, it could be bought without prescription). It even made its way into confectionery.

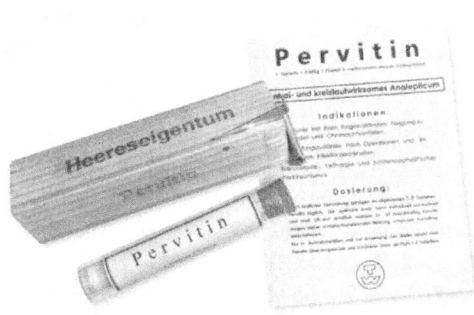

"Hildebrand chocolates are always a delight," went the slogan. Girls were recommended to eat two or three, after which they would be able to get through their housework in no time at all – with the bonus that they would also lose weight, given the deleterious effect Pervitin had on the appetite.

Cocaine, opium, and marijuana were in common use by the elite who craved the dope to enhance their sexual stimulation, and Hitler was begging twice a day for another injection of the haphazard melange of vitamins, hormones, methamphetamine, oxycodone and sometimes morphine which had kept him functioning throughout the war. Back in the occupied territories, concentration camp doctors performed characteristically cruel scientific experiments on Jewish inmates at Dachau and Auschwitz, forcing groups to march in circles without sleep for days to determine whether cocaine or meth was a better stimulant for soldiers.

Workers at the Temmler factory in Berlin produced tablets of Pervitin for the German army and Luftwaffe in 1940. Photograph: Temmler Pharma GmbH & Co.

Naturally, it wasn't long before soldiers were relying on it. And writing home begging their families to send them Pervitin, the only way they knew to fight the great enemy without sleep. In Berlin, it was the job of Dr Otto Ranke, the director of the Institute for General and Defence Physiology, to protect the Wehrmacht's "animated machines", its soldiers from "wear and tear" after conducting some tests he concluded that Pervitin was indeed excellent medicine for exhausted soldiers. Not only did it prevent unnecessary sleep, chemists, who would become addicted to the drug, observed that they could work for 50 hours on Pervitin without feeling fatigued. It also switched off inhibitions, making fighting easier, or, at any rate, less terrifying. In 1940, as plans were made to invade France through the Ardennes mountains, a "stimulant decree" was sent out to army doctors, recommending that soldiers take one tablet per day, two at night in short sequence, and another one or two tablets after two or three hours if necessary. The Wehrmacht ordered 35 million tablets for the army and Luftwaffe, and the Temmler factory increased production.

The success of Blitzkrieg was largely the result of the Wehrmacht's reliance on crystal meth. The invasion of France was made possible by the drugs. No drugs, no invasion. When Hitler heard about the plan to invade through Ardennes, he loved it knowing the allies were massed in northern Belgium. But the high command said:" it's not possible, at night we have to rest, and the allies will retreat, and we will be stuck in the mountains". But then the stimulant decree was released, and that enabled them to stay awake for three days and three nights. Rommel and all those tank commanders were high, and without Pervitin the tanks wouldn't have moved and, they certainly wouldn't have won."

Hitler appointed Heinrich Himmler, seen here in Luxembourg as military commander and later Commander of the Replacement (Home) Army and General Plenipotentiary for the administration of the entire Third Reich (Generalbevollmächtigter für die

Verwaltung). Specifically, he was given command of the Army Group Upper Rhine.

Overall, around 10,000 Luxembourgers were conscripted into the German armed forces. Over a third of them refused to wear the German uniform, driving them underground, often with disastrous consequences for their families, as the occupying forces responded to any form of opposition with torture, beatings and terror: deportations to the east, imprisonment in concentration camps (Hinzert camp in particular) and executions. It was the Jewish community that particularly suffered at the hands of the Nazi regime. Among the 4,000 Jewish people living in Luxembourg before the war (approximately 25% of which were Luxembourgers, the remaining being refugees from other European countries), over 90% never saw the country again. A third were killed. Groups of Luxembourgers who sometimes came from the scouting movement or disbanded political parties gradually organised themselves to fight against the occupation. In its initial stage, this "Resistance" organised the smuggling of fugitives and allied aviators who escaped prison to French and Belgian resistance groups, as well as the dissimulation of Luxembourgish members of the resistance, and the printing and distribution of anti-Nazi literature of which our Anthony was in control of production.

For months the maelstrom of inappropriate behaviour by the German officers within the confines of the Alfa had become unacceptable. Carpet bombing of Berlin was leading to an exodus of political figures to different cities within the occupied nations. Leading Nazi figures such as Himmler, Goebbels, and Speer could be expected to relocate in the Grand Duchy at any time. The owner of the hotel Alfred Lefèvre insisted that the bawdy officers be located elsewhere or be prohibited from gathering in the public rooms. Fearful of reprisals from the German High Command for both the owner and the Luxembourg garrison was agreed.

The Hotel Alfa Luxembourg on Place de la Gare was built in 1930 by the owner Alfred Lefèvre according to the plans of the architect Léon Bouvart. The historic building adjacent was classified a national monument in May 1991 and is since then listed among the "Inventory of Buildings Worthy of Protection of Luxembourg". The Alfa Luxembourg Hotel owes its official recognition as a cultural monument to its unique zigzag-style facade, with its typical ornaments, geometric motifs and triangular balconies, all expressions of the Art Deco style. Inside the building one finds precious landscape paintings by Julien Lefèvre, son of the owner Alfred Lefèvre. Julien Lefèvre (1907-1984) is one of the most significant painters and sculptors of Luxembourg. Large companies such as the Compagnie des Grands Vins de Champagne E. Mercier or the tobacco and cigarette manufacturer Heintz Van Landewyck settled in the station's proximity and trumped each other with buildings of high artistic and historical value. (With its daring, modern interior and its legendary jazz and variety shows, the Hotel Alfa enjoyed a powerful attraction before World War II becoming one of the major meeting places in the capital.

Therefore, it is no surprise that the Grand Hotel served as quarters for the American generals George Patton and Omar Bradley from late 1944. Dwight Eisenhower, the journalist and writer Martha Gellhorn (at that time the wife of Ernest Hemmingway), Winston Churchill and other celebrities also stayed here, turning the Alfa Hotel into a place of legendary meetings and celebrations.)

In the spring of 1943, the Alfa was to have a rather unusual celebrity guest and his wife. William and Margaret Joyce each had their own rooms on separate floors and would only meet up when it was time to do their radio broadcasts using the excellent and all-powerful studios and transmitters formally assigned to the English language service of Radio Luxembourg.

William Joyce (Lord Haw Haw) was there with his mistresses Gerta and Lisa, and Margaret with Nicky von Besack and a bevy of beefcake gigolos.

By now casual sex in Germany was the norm, with those unable to resist, copulation in public was to be seen everywhere. Erotic acts had taken possession of everybody especially women who had discarded all modesty, in a mixture of apathy and pleasure seeking.

This had been mirrored in the German Officers behaviour at the Alfa, but not anymore! Although Margaret encouraged an audience, William was too embarrassed to exhibit his performance.

Each morning William Joyce would take breakfast with Oberleutnant Anton Heidelberg, with Anthony ensuring that he communicated with Joyce in English mimicking an Anglo-German Accent. Both enjoyed each other's company.

German Army Guards policing the entrance to the Villa Louvigny housing the studios of the French. German and English services, now taken over by the Minister of Propaganda Joseph Goebbels.

Footnote: When the Wehrmacht invaded Luxembourg on the 10 May 1940, the C.L.R. immediately stopped broadcasting. To prevent the invaders from using the powerful transmitters as propaganda tools, much of the broadcasting equipment was taken to France. While this gained some time, the Nazis soon repaired the antennas and started broadcasting towards Great Britain.

In the final days of the Nazi occupation, the stations in Junlinster and the Villa Louvigny narrowly escaped destruction. Before much damage was done, the Allies captured the station and quickly turned the antenna towards their recently departed occupants. This time, the propaganda shows featured among others anti-nazi jokes and were meant to undermine support for Hitler among German civilians.

"Hello world. Here is Radio Luxembourg". These were the opening words when the English service of Radio Luxembourg resumed independent broadcasting on 12 November 1945. The new schedule clearly set itself apart from the precedent program launching new programs including a show dedicated to Luxembourgish songs.

CHAPTER SEVEN: LORD HAW HAW aka WILLIAM JOYCE

What led him to become one of the most recognizable Axis broadcasters during the Second World War? What drove Joyce, a man of Anglo-Irish descent, to become a turncoat and willingly collude with the Nazis?

To fully understand William Joyce's story, just look as his early life. Joyce was born in New York City on 26 April 1906, to British parents. His father, Michael Francis Joyce, was a naturalised US citizen of Irish origin, and his mother, Gertrude Emily Brooke, was from an Anglo-Irish family. However, Joyce's time in the United States was short-lived. His family moved to Galway, Ireland when William was three years old, and Joyce grew up in the county.

William Brooke Joyce was born on Herkimer Street in Brooklyn, New York, United States. His father was Michael Francis Joyce, an Irish Catholic from a family of tenant farmers in Ballinrobe, County Mayo, who had acquired U.S. citizenship in 1894. His mother was Gertrude Emily Brooke, who although she was born in Shaw, near Oldham in Lancashire, it was obvious she from a well-off Anglican Anglo-Irish family of physicians associated with County Roscommon. A few years after William's birth, the family returned to Salthill, County Galway. Joyce attended Coláiste Iognáid, a Jesuit school in County Galway, from 1915 to 1921. His parents were unionist and hostile to republicanism. His mother was a devout Protestant, and there were tensions between her and her family because she married a Catholic.

In 1921, during the Irish War of Independence, he was recruited by the British Army as a courier and was almost assassinated by the IRA on his way home from school. He was suspected by the Irish Republican Army of working as an informant for the Black and Tans; which could have had extremely serious consequences in 1920-21." On 14 November 1920, the Catholic priest and republican sympathiser Michael Griffin was abducted and murdered by members of the Auxiliary Division, and Joyce was further suspected of being involved in his murder. Keating eventually arranged for Joyce to be enlisted into the Worcestershire

Regiment, moving him out of harm's way in Ireland by transferring him to the Norton Barracks in England where the regiment was stationed. However, Joyce was discharged a few months later when it was discovered that he was just 15.

Joyce continued his education in England, and briefly attended King's College School, Wimbledon. His family followed him to England two years later. Joyce had relatives in Birkenhead, Merseyside, whom he visited on a few occasions eventually enrolling at Birkbeck College where he entered the Officer Training Corps. At Birkbeck he obtained a first-class honours degree in English. After graduating he applied for a job in the Foreign Office, but was rejected and took a job as a school teacher. William developed an interest in fascism and worked with, but never joined, the British Fascists of Rotha Lintorn-Orman. On 22 October 1924, while stewarding a meeting in support of Conservative Party candidate Jack Lazarus ahead of the 1924 general election,] Joyce was attacked by communists and received a deep razor slash across his right cheek. It left a permanent scar which ran from the earlobe to the corner of the mouth. While Joyce often said that his attackers were Jewish, historian Colin Holmes claims that Joyce's first wife told him that "it wasn't a Jewish Communist who disfigured him .... He was knifed by an Irish woman".

 Following his injury, William Joyce proceeded to climb up the ranks of fascist organizations in Britain. He joined Oswald Mosley's British Union of Fascists in 1932, distinguishing himself as a brilliant speaker.

Eventually, however, Joyce was sacked by Mosley after the 1937 London County Council elections. Furious, he split off from the BUF to form his own political party to be known as the National Socialist League. More virulently anti-Semitic than the BUF, the NSL aimed to integrate German Nazism into British society to create a new form of British fascism. By 1939 however, the other leaders of the NSL had opposed Joyce's efforts, opting to model the organization on German Nazism. Embittered, Joyce turned to alcoholism and dissolved the National Socialist League, which turned out to be a fateful decision. (He had to get out of the UK having been tipped off that the British authorities intended to detain him under Defence

Regulation 18B. He would become a naturalised German citizen in 1940.) William Joyce travelled to Germany with his second wife, Margaret, in late August 1939. However, the groundwork for his departure had been made a year earlier. Joyce obtained a British passport in 1938 by falsely claiming he was a British subject when he was an American citizen. When he eventually travelled to Berlin, Joyce could not find employment in Berlin until a chance meeting with Dorothy Eckersley.

Dorothy, through her contacts was able to get him an audition at the Berlin equivalent to the BBC's Broadcasting House. Eckersley was the former wife or second wife of the chief engineer of the BBC, Peter Eckersley. Despite having a heavy cold and having almost lost his voice, Joyce was recruited immediately for radio announcements and scriptwriting at German radio's English service. His first broadcast was reading the news in English on 6 September 1939, just three days after the declaration of war between Britain and Germany. On 18 September he received a contract as a newsreader. After the dismissal of Norman Baillie-Stewart in December, Joyce became the principal reader of news and the writer of six talks a week, thus becoming the station's best-known propaganda broadcaster recruited by Joseph Goebbels' Reich Ministry of Propaganda and given his own radio show, "Germany Calling." Goebbels needed foreign fascists to spread Nazi propaganda to Allied countries, especially Britain and America, and Joyce was the ideal candidate.

In a newspaper article of 14 September 1939, the radio critic Jonah Barrington of the Daily Express wrote of hearing a gent "moaning periodically from Zeesen" who "speaks English of the haw-haw, damit-get-out-of-my-way variety". Four days later he gave him the nickname "Lord Haw-Haw".

The voice Barrington heard is widely believed to be that of Wolf Mittler, a German journalist whose near-flawless English sounded like a caricature of an upper-crust Englishman.

However, Mittler only made five or six broadcasts and was quickly replaced by other broadcasters, leading to uncertainty over to whom Barrington had been referring. When Joyce became the most prominent broadcaster of Nazi propaganda by the end of 1939, the name stuck to him. Joyce himself began to trade on the notoriety of the nickname more than a year later, on 3 April 1941, when he announced himself as "William Joyce, otherwise known as Lord Haw-Haw". His initial broadcasts were focused on inciting distrust within the British public towards their government. Joyce tried to convince the British people that the British working class was being oppressed by a nefarious alliance between the middle class and Jewish businessmen of the upper class, which had control of the government. Additionally, Joyce used a segment called "Schmidt and Smith" to relay his propaganda. A German colleague of Joyce's would assume the role of Schmidt, while Joyce would portray Smith, an Englishman. The two would then engage in discussions about Britain, with Joyce continuing his previous pattern of degrading and attacking the British government, people, and way of life. During one broadcast, Joyce exclaimed:

"The whole system of English so-called democracy is a fraud. It is an elaborate system of make-believe, under which you may have the illusion that you are choosing your own government, but which simply ensures that the same privileged class, the same wealthy people, shall rule England under different names... Your nation is controlled... by big business... newspaper proprietors, Jewish bankers, opportunist statesmen... men like Churchill... Camrose and Rothermere".

As was said, Joyce's broadcasts initially came from studios in Berlin, later being transferred (because of heavy Allied bombing) to Luxembourg City and finally to Alpen near Hamburg, and were relayed over a network of German-controlled radio stations in Zeesen, Hamburg, Bremen, Luxembourg, Hilversum and Calais

Joyce also broadcast on and wrote scripts for the other German propaganda stations including Büro Concordia organisation, which ran several black propaganda stations, many of which pretended to broadcast illegally from within Britain. His role in writing the scripts increased over time, and German radio capitalised on his public persona. Initially an anonymous broadcaster, Joyce eventually revealed his real name to his listeners, and he would occasionally be announced as, "William Joyce, otherwise known as Lord Haw-Haw". Urban legends soon circulated about Lord Haw-Haw, alleging that the broadcaster was well-informed about political and military events to the point of near-omniscience. In the summer of 1942, it was decided that he should no longer read the news and, from then on, he read only his own talks in "Views on the News".

Listening to Joyce's broadcasts was officially discouraged but was not illegal, and many Britons tuned in. There was a desire by civilian listeners to hear what the other side was saying, as information during wartime was strictly censored. At the height of his influence, in 1940, Joyce had an estimated six million regular and 18 million occasional listeners in the UK. The broadcasts always began with the announcer's words, "Germany calling, Germany calling, Germany calling". These broadcasts urged the British people to surrender and were well known for their jeering, sarcastic and menacing tone.

The Reich Security Main Office commissioned Joyce to give lectures at the University of Berlin for SS members in the winter of 1941–42 on the topic of "British fascism and acute questions concerning the British world empire".

Thanks to Joyce's caustic rhetoric, British audiences found "Germany Calling" to be quality entertainment. Joyce's dramatic, fiery oratory was much more entertaining than the sombre, dry programming of the BBC, and his show became a hit. He was given the moniker of "Lord Haw-Haw" in 1939 by the British press because of "the sneering character of his speech."

By 1940, it was estimated that "Germany Calling" had six million regular listeners and 18 million occasional listeners in the United Kingdom. Joseph Goebbels was immensely pleased by Joyce's broadcasts. He wrote in his diary, "I tell the Führer about Lord Haw-Haw's success, which is really astonishing." For the first couple of years of his broadcasts for most households it became compelling listening, and at work women would talk about his nonsense during their canteen breaks, but soldiers never tuned in.

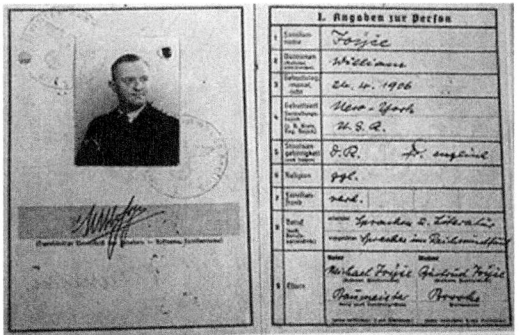

In recognition of his success, Joyce was given a pay raise and was promoted to the chief commentator for all of the English Services.

While Lord Haw-Haw's broadcasts focused on undermining the British confidence in their government during the first year of the war, things changed when Nazi Germany invaded Denmark, Norway, and France in April and May of 1940. Joyce's propaganda became even more violent. It emphasized Germany's military might, threatened Britain with invasion, and urged the country to surrender. Eventually, British citizens came to see Joyce's broadcasts not as entertainment, but as legitimate threats to Britain and the Allies. Despite Lord Haw-Haw's best efforts, his incendiary propaganda only had a minimal impact on British morale during the Second World War. Listeners grew tired of Joyce's constant contempt for and sarcasm about Britain and took his propaganda less seriously. Joyce continued broadcasting from Germany throughout the war, moving from Berlin to other cities and towns to avoid Allied bombing raids. He eventually settled in Hamburg, where he remained until May 1945.

Joyce was captured by British forces on 28 May, transported to England, and put on trial. Joyce was convicted of high treason and sentenced to death on 19 September 1945. The court argued that since Joyce possessed a British passport between 10 September 1939, and 2 July 1940, he owed his allegiance to Great Britain. Since Joyce served Nazi Germany during that time as well, the court concluded that he had betrayed his country and therefore committed high treason. After being found guilty, Joyce was taken to Wandsworth Prison and hanged on 3 January 1946.

William Joyce's story is one of contradictions. Joyce had to reconcile his identity as a Briton, an Irishman, an Englishman, and an American due to his transitory upbringing. His search for meaning led him to fascism, which laid out the structure for the rest of his life. Ironically, Joyce's adoption of fascism led to his downfall. His obsession with Nazi ideology blinded him to the fact that he betrayed his countrymen and his identity, and, as a result, he paid the ultimate price.

End of the road: crowds gathered outside the gates of HMP Wandsworth, after William Joyce's execution, in January 1946. He was the penultimate person hanged for a crime other than murder in the United Kingdom. The last was Theodore Schurch, executed for treachery the following day also in London at Pentonville Prison. In both cases, the hangman was Albert Pierrepoint. Joyce died an "Anglican", like his mother, despite a long and friendly correspondence with a Roman Catholic priest who fought hard for William's soul.

The scar on Joyce's face split wide open because of the pressure applied to his head upon his drop from the gallows. As was customary for executed criminals, Joyce's remains were buried in an unmarked grave within the walls of Wandsworth Prison. In 1976, following a campaign by his daughter, Heather Iandolo, his body was reinterred in New Cemetery, Galway, as he had lived in Galway with his family from 1909 until 1922. Despite the ambiguity of his religious allegiances, he was given a Roman Catholic Tridentine Mass. Heather Iandolo died aged 93 in August 2022 having devoted much of her life to atoning for the sins of her father.

CHAPTER EIGHT

AUTUMN LEAVES

From late 1942 German strategy, every feature of which was determined by Hitler, was solely aimed at protecting the still very large area under German control, most of Europe and part of North Africa; against a future Soviet onslaught on the Eastern Front and against future Anglo-U.S. offensives on the southern and western fronts. The Germans' vague hopes that the Allies would shrink from such costly tasks or that the "unnatural" coalition of Western capitalism and Soviet Communism would break up before achieving victory were disappointed, so Hitler, in accordance with his dictum that "Germany shall either be a world power or not be at all," consciously resolved to preside over the downfall of the German nation. He gave inflexible orders whereby whole armies were made to stand their ground in tactically hopeless positions and were forbidden to surrender under any circumstances.

The initial success of this strategy, in preventing a German rout during the Soviet winter counteroffensive of 1941–42, had blinded Hitler to its impracticability in the very different military circumstances on the Eastern Front. By 1943 the Germans simply lacked enough troops to defend an extremely long front against much more numerous Soviet forces. The horrors of being sent to the Eastern front meant instant death for 70% of Hitler's war weary troops. In those months, it was apparent that Hitler's strategy, from a political standpoint, remained inexplicable to most Western historians. To strengthen the German forces in western Europe at the expense of those on the Eastern Front was simply cannot-fodder in the extreme. In view of the danger of the great Anglo-U.S. invasion of western Europe the loss of some part of his eastern conquests evidently seemed to Hitler to be less serious. Hitler continued to insist on the primacy of the war in the west.

The strategy of keeping his armies stationary was made easier for Hitler by the complete ascendancy he had achieved over his generals, who disputed with Hitler only at the risk of losing their commands or worse. Frequent changes were made in the command of the various army groups and armies, with the result that during 1943 most of the talented commanders who had been associated with Germany's past successes were removed, and everyone who was suspected of a critical attitude at headquarters was executed.

The gossip around Luxembourg was toxic. Mass murder of locals was any everyday occurrence, though no one really knew why as those with any contacts had already been helped to leave the city .

Dr Agnese Semjonova and her husband the Latvia lothario Jānis approached Oberleutnant Anton Heidelberg with an unexpected proposition from Maria an Alfa kitchen assistant and her 15 year old daughter Monique. They arranged to meet Anton in Jānis' treatment room.

"I have watched you Oberleutnant and you seem to be different from the other officers who are resident here from time to time. You are not taking part in their group sexual activities though for me, I have no choice. It has become a way of life a way of survival, and I enjoy the thrill even though I despise those who have stolen my country. My daughter Monique will have to join the party soon and we have both discussed that we would like you to take her virginity and play with her so that she knows what to expect".

Anton is speechless, but before he has time to compose himself Maria undresses her daughter proving that Monique is or is becoming a woman, explaining as disrobes the young lady that coitus interruptus prior to ejaculation with the penis inserted swiftly into the mouth will give the assailant an unexpected double orgasmic sensation. Also, it will, hopefully, prevent pregnancy.

When admiring Monique's feminine charms he chirps up, "You both have the same hair colour, but Monique has a well-developed black bush. She will be raped and then have her throat cut because she is a Jew, and I guess so too are you, Maria."

"I am not Jewish! The father of my daughter is a Jew! Or should I say was a Jew. I was a young girl when they took me in as a house maid. Mr and Mrs van Ryn were very kind to me. Rhita van Ryn was severely disabled, and she asked me, as I am asking you on behalf of my daughter; if I would have sex with her husband with hope that he would father a child. When the Germans occupied Luxembourg in May 1940 everything changed. There was house to house searches to identify Jews, and being disabled Rhita was dragged into the street in her bed clothes and full public view executed in front of her husband. Marteen van Ryn was ordered back into the house. "As soon as I became pregnant Marteen gave me an apartment and when Monique was born the Ryn family paid for a nursemaid, so everything looked normal, and I was able to remain their housemaid. We were in our apartment when Rhita was murdered, and my daughter and Marteen's of course, was just 12."

Maria continues "Marteen and I prolonged our intimacy, as Rhita would have wanted, and I really believed that, until he was interned by the Gestapo within the Villa Pauly (above), after then we heard that he had been moved to Łódź in the very west of Germany not too far from the Luxembourg border".

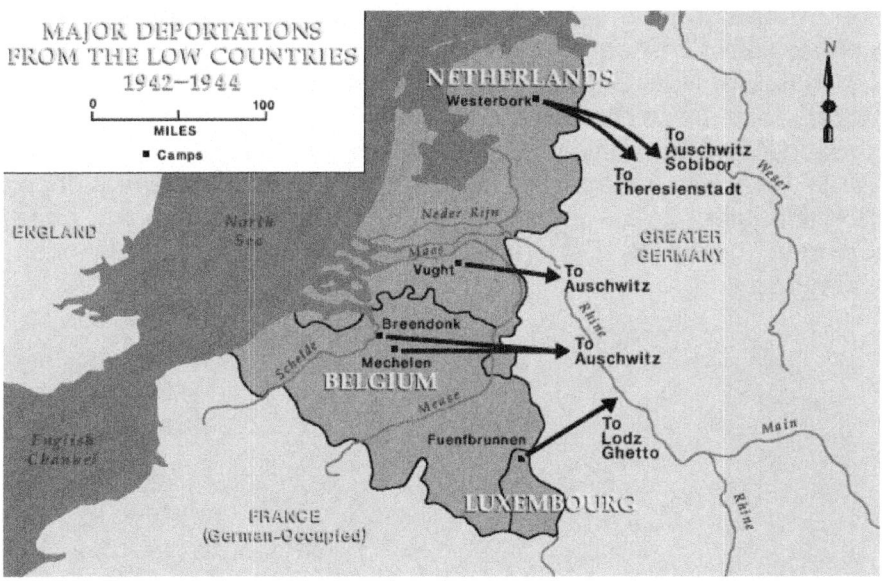

The Łódź Ghetto or Litzmannstadt Ghetto (after the Nazi German name for Łódź) was a Nazi ghetto established by the German authorities for Jews and Roma. It was the second-largest ghetto in all of German-occupied Europe after the Warsaw Ghetto. Situated in the city of Łódź, and originally intended as a preliminary step upon a more extensive plan of creating the "Judenfrei" provinces that included Luxembourg and Warthegau, the ghetto was transformed into a new major industrial centre, manufacturing war supplies for Nazi Germany and especially for the Wehrmacht. The number of people incarcerated in it was increased further by the Jews deported from Nazi-controlled territories. As early as 30 April 1940, when the gates we intended to be closed on the ghetto, it housed 163,777 residents. Because of its remarkable productivity, the ghetto managed to survive until August 1944.

"Sadly, we expect that the love of my life Marteen didn't survive. He was employed in one of our country's financial institutions connected to the Banque de Luxembourg, I think. Before he was no longer permitted to work he gave me $2,000 US, a handful of British Sovereigns and a money bank bag of very old Swedish Gold Kronor, which always puzzled me because Marteen told me that Oscar II, was born on 28 January 1829 in Stockholm and died 8 December 1907 also in Stockholm was the King of Sweden from 1872 to 1907 and of Norway from 1872 to 1905. Sweden insisted on being paid in gold coins when Germany purchased Swedish iron ore which was an important economic and military factor in the European theatre of World War II, as Sweden was the main contributor of iron ore to Nazi Germany. The average percentages by source of Nazi Germany's iron ore procurement through 1933–43 by source were: Sweden: a staggering 48% Domestic production (Germany): 22% and elsewhere by confiscation 30%. Within the German military the Navy was most dependent on Swedish steel as an absolute necessity to the German war effort, Sweden, being like Portugal, Switzerland and the Irish Republic being "neutral".

"Of course it is now illegal, punishable by death squad, for anyone to own such foreign assets. I am trusting you my friend Anton not only with the body of my beautiful daughter but with both of our lives. Make love to me Anton so that Monique can watch and learn – we will be forever in your debt."

At this point Dr Agnese Semjonova interjected saying that she would take care of the bleaching of Moniques black bush and her very fetching whisps of under-arm hair. She also added, "Anton, I don't believe you are a German officer, but please I don't want to or need to know your pedigree. What I will say is, if you betray us in any way, you will be dead in under a minute. Also, I understand you have a huge quantity of Reichsmarks."

"Many of the shops here are going to cease their trading in six weeks, and go underground, so buy everything that you can to use up some of your German currency. We hear that the Americans are preparing with Montgomery to destroy the Nazi control of the Ardennes, though that won't be until 1944 I guess."

"In the meantime, this naughty Doctor Agnese and my man-child are leaving you now, so the handsome Anton go fuck the lovely Maria and the delicious young Monique und das ist ein Befehl ! We are only next door, and we will be listening. And Maria our young man is circumcised – make of that what you will!"

Maria was in a mind-set of making the experience a romantic passionate encounter, but there was no reason to act. She was swept up in the emotion and not at all inhibited by having her daughter in full view of her eroticism. Anton too was fully primed his libido enhanced by a little yellow pill prescribed by the good doctor. He had never been able to sustain his pleasures before and was such a satisfying and unique opportunity for the couple.

Anton avoided looking at Monique though Maria devoured her daughter's delight at watching and learning and being arouse by a delicate exhibition of love, passion, and pleasure. The young lady was already on the verge and having eye to eye contact with her little girl seeing several real orgasms erupt from her mum she whispered in English "come on Anton fake an orgasm and take on deflowering Monique!"

The change over was instant with Monique's lovely legs already open and eager to take her first sip from the cup of life.

This wasn't a bloodless coup, but it was painless. There was a dull sound as Monique's hymen was torn but already excessively self-lubricated the full sex act was pure perfection. Both were "blooded" but that added to the excitement and didn't prevent oral activity during the act. Unexpectedly Monique had her first ever orgasm swiftly followed by a second. She couldn't get enough. The petting the kissing the penetration and the loving were all exemplary. She enjoyed every moment and activity especially the added glimpses of her mummy pleasuring herself.

 It was time for Monique to take her second sip from the cup of life as she took his manhood in hand, just as her mother had explained, and hand-milked Anton into her pert lips and into her deep throat as he released his love potion.

A sexual success which was repeated as often as needed which became very frequent. Love was in the air, but with the war moving on self-preservation and Reichsmark exchanges too became a priority. And what makes this love affair so special was the generosity of Maria as she hidden Sovereigns stitched into Anton's clothing – not in the hems or collar but within the cut of the armpit, making it almost impossible to locate during a physical search.

Would they ever meet again, would they and Mr & Mrs Doctor all survive? The very thought of such a loss of anyone of them from this unique team was an emotion not to be contemplate.

CHAPTER NINE

READ ALL ABOUT IT

Honolulu Star-Bulletin 1st EXTRA

8 PAGES—HONOLULU, TERRITORY OF HAWAII, U. S. A., SUNDAY, DECEMBER 7, 1941—8 PAGES   + PRICE FIVE CENTS

WAR!

(Associated Press by Transpacific Telephone)

SAN FRANCISCO, Dec. 7.— President Roosevelt announced this morning that Japanese planes had attacked Manila and Pearl Harbor.

OAHU BOMBED BY JAPANESE PLANES

SIX KNOWN DEAD, 21 INJURED, AT EMERGENCY HOSPITAL

Attack Made On Island's Defense Areas

WASHINGTON, Dec. 7.—Text of a White House announcement detailing the attack on the Hawaiian islands is:

"The Japanese attacked Pearl Harbor from the air and all naval and military activities on the Island of Oahu, principal American base in the Hawaiian islands."

Oahu was attacked at 7:55 this morning by Japanese planes.

The Rising Sun, emblem of Japan, was seen on plane wing tips.

Wave after wave of bombers streamed through the clouded morning sky from the southwest and flung their missiles on a city resting in peaceful Sabbath calm.

According to an unconfirmed report received at the governor's office, the Japanese force that attacked Oahu reached island waters aboard two small airplane carriers.

It was also reported that at the governor's office an attempt had been made to bomb the USS Lexington, or that it had been bombed.

CITY IN UPROAR

Within 10 minutes the city was in an uproar. As bombs fell in many parts of the city, and in defense areas the defenders of the islands went into quick action.

Army intelligence officers at Ft. Shafter announced officially shortly after 9 a. m. the fact of the bombardment by an enemy but hnng previous army and navy had taken immediate measures in defense.

"Oahu is under a sporadic air raid," the announcement said.

"Civilians are ordered to stay off the streets until further notice."

CIVILIANS ORDERED OFF STREETS

The army has ordered that all civilians stay off the streets and highways and not use telephones.

Evidence that the Japanese attack has registered some hits was shown by three billowing pillars of smoke in the Pearl Harbor and Hickam field area.

All navy personnel and civilian defense workers, with the exception of women, have been ordered to duty at Pearl Harbor.

The Pearl Harbor highway was immediately a mass of racing cars.

A trickling stream of injured people began pouring into the city emergency hospital a few minutes after the bombardment started.

Thousands of telephone calls almost swamped the Mutual Telephone Co., which put extra operators on duty.

At The Star-Bulletin office the phone calls deluged the single operator and it was impossible for this newspaper, for sometime, to handle the flood of calls. Here also an emergency operator was called.

HOUR OF ATTACK: 7:55 A. M.

An official army report from department headquarters, made public shortly before 11, five secretary of t he major disaster council, tive secretary of the first attack was at 7.55 a. m.

Witnesses that saw at least 50 airplanes over Pearl Harbor.

The attack centered in the Pearl Harbor. Army authorities said:

"The rising sun was seen on the wing tips of the airplanes.

Although martial law has not been declared officially, the city of Honolulu was operating under M-Day conditions.

It is reliably reported that Wheeler field Hickam field, Kaneohe bay and naval air station and Pearl Harbor.

Some enemy planes were reported shot down.

The body of the pilot was seen in a plane burning at Wahiawa.

Oahu appeared to be taking calmly after the first uproar of queries.

ANTIAIRCRAFT GUNS IN ACTION

First indication of the raid came shortly before 8 this morning when antiaircraft guns around Pearl Harbor began sending up a thunderous barrage.

At the same time a vast cloud of black smoke arose from the naval base and also from Hickam field where flames could be seen.

BOMB NEAR GOVERNOR'S MANSION

Shortly before 9:30 a bomb fell near Washington Place, the residence of the governor. Governor Poindexter and Secretary Charles M. Hite were there.

It was reported that the bomb killed an unidentified Chinese man across the street in front of the Schuman Carriage Co. where windows were broken.

C. E. Daniels, a welder, found a fragment of shell or bomb at South and Queen Sts. which he brought into the City Hall. This fragment weighed about a pound.

At 10:05 a. m. today Governor Poindexter telephoned to The Star-Bulletin announcing he has declared a state of emergency for the entire territory.

He announced that Edward L. Doty, executive secretary of the major disaster council, has been appointed director under the M-Day law's provisions.

Governor Poindexter urged all residents of Honolulu to remain off the street, and the people of the territory to remain calm.

Mr. Doty reported that all major disaster council wardens and medical units were on duty within a half hour of the time the alarm was given.

Workers employed at Pearl Harbor were ordered at 10:10 a. m. not to report at Pearl Harbor.

The mayor's major disaster council was to meet at the city hall at about 10:30 this morning.

At least two Japanese planes were reported of Hawaiian department headquarters to have been shot down.

One of the planes was shot down at Ft. Kamehameha and the other back of the Wa—

Turn to Page 2, Column 1, move.

Hundreds See City Bombed

Hundreds of Honolulans who hurried to the top of Punchbowl soon after battle began to look out over the whole panorama of surprise attack and defense.

Names of Dead and Injured

The city emergency hospital reported at 10:30 a list of 6 killed and 21 injured.

Turn to Page 2, Column 2

Schools Closed

All schools on Oahu both public and private will remain closed Monday.

Turn to Page 2, Column 6

Editorial

HAWAII MEETS THE CRISIS

Honolulu and Hawaii will meet the emergency of war today as Honolulu and Hawaii have met emergencies in the past: coolly, calmly and with fortitude and complete support of the officials, officers and troops who are in charge.

Governor Poindexter and the army and navy leaders have called upon the public to remain calm, for civilians who have no essential business on the streets to stay off, and for every man and woman to do his duty.

That request, coupled with the measures promptly taken to avert the situation that has suddenly and terribly developed, will be needed.

Hawaii will do its part as a loyal American territory. In this crisis, every difference of race, creed and color will be submerged in the war desire and determination to play the part that Americans always play in crises.

BULLETIN

Additional Star-Bulletin extras today will cover the latest developments in this war move.

When World War II began in September 1939 with Germany's invasion of Poland and Britain and France's declaration of war on Germany, Roosevelt sought ways to assist Britain militarily. Churchill pleaded with the USA to support the UK, which after the Nazi's occupied all of Europe with Britain standing alone.

Isolationist leaders like Charles Lindbergh and Senator William Borah successfully mobilized opposition to Roosevelt's proposed repeal of the Neutrality Act, but Roosevelt won Congressional approval of the sale of arms on a cash-and-carry basis. He also began regular secret correspondences with Britain's First Lord of the Admiralty, Winston Churchill, in September 1939—the first of 1,700 letters and telegrams between them. Roosevelt forged a close personal relationship with Churchill, who became Prime Minister of the United Kingdom in May 1940. The Fall of France in June 1940 shocked the American public, and isolationist sentiment declined. By July 1940, Roosevelt appointed two interventionist Republican leaders, Mr Henry L. Stimson and Mr Frank Knox, as Secretaries of War and the Navy, respectively. Both parties gave support to his plans for a rapid build-up of the American military, but the isolationists warned that Roosevelt would get the nation into an unnecessary war with Germany. Britain was fighting Nazi Germany alone, and all Roosevelt could do was hire out to the Brits a bunch of retired US navy battle ships under their Lend-Lease terms, a debt which the UK was paying off in huge tranches right up until 2006.

New York World-Telegram

7TH SPORTS
LATEST RACING
Results on Page 36.

PRICE THREE CENTS

VOL. 74—NO. 135.—IN TWO SECTIONS—SECTION ONE   NEW YORK, MONDAY, DECEMBER 8, 1941.

1500 DEAD IN HAWAII

Congress Votes War on Japan; Manila Bases Bombed Again

Tally in Senate Is 82 to 0. In House 388 to 1, with Miss Rankin Sole Objector

100 to 200 Soldiers Killed in Japanese Raid On Luzon in Philippines

Yes, for three years we Brits stood alone after all of mainland Europe, including our beloved Channel Islands, was occupied by the Nazis. All that changed when Japan bombed the US navy at anchor in Pearl Harbor, and the United States declared war on

Japan, and Germany then declaring war on the USA. The U.S. Pacific Fleet had been stationed at Pearl Harbor since April 1940. In addition to nearly 100 naval vessels, including 8 battleships, there were substantial military and air forces. As the tension mounted, Admiral Husband Kimmel and Lieutenant General Walter Short, who shared command at Pearl Harbor, were warned of the possibility of war, specifically on 16 October and again on 24 and 27 November 1940. The notice of November 27, to Kimmel, began, "This despatch is to be considered a war warning," went on to say that "negotiations have ceased," and directed the admiral to "execute an appropriate defensive deployment." Kimmel also was ordered to "undertake such reconnaissance and other measures as you deem necessary." The communication of the same day to Short declared that "hostile action is possible at any moment" and, like its naval counterpart, urged "measures of reconnaissance."

In response to these warnings, the measures taken by the army and navy commanders were, as the event proved, far from adequate. Short ordered an alert against sabotage and concentrated most of his fighter planes at the base on Wheeler Field in an effort to prevent damage to them. He also gave orders to operate five of the mobile radar sets that had been set up in the island from 4:00 AM to 7:00 AM, considered to be the most dangerous period. (Unlike in Britain, US Radar training, however, was in a far-from-advanced stage.)

Kimmel, even though his intelligence had not been able to locate substantial elements in the Japanese fleet, especially the first-line ships in carrier divisions 1 and 2 did not expand his reconnaissance activities to the northwest, the logical point for an attack. He moored the entire fleet (save that part which was at sea) in the harbour and permitted a part of his personnel to go on shore leave. Neither of these officers suspected that the base at Pearl Harbor would itself be subjected to attack. Nor, for that matter, is there any indication that their superiors in Washington were in any way conscious of the approaching danger. In the ten days between the war warning of 27 November and the Japanese attack itself, no additional action was taken by Washington.

Early on Sunday morning, 7 December, Washington learned that the Japanese ambassadors had been instructed to ask for an interview with the secretary of state at 1:00pm (7:30pm Pearl Harbor time). This was a clear indication that war was at hand. The message took some time to decode, and it was not in the hands of the chief of naval operations until about 10:30. It was delivered to the War Department between 9:00 and 10:00am. General George Marshall, the U.S. Army chief of staff, was out horseback riding and did not see the dispatch until he arrived at his office about 11:15am. The chief of naval operations, Admiral Harold Stark, even then did not think that the communication called for any additional instructions to Kimmel. However, Marshall did decide to send a new warning and gave orders to the military command to communicate with the navy. He did not telephone, fearing that his words might be intercepted, and instead sent his dispatch by telegram. There was a mix-up in communication, however, and the warning did not reach Hawaii until after the attack had begun. It is important to note that it had not been filed until noon, only an hour before the Japanese planes moved in on the base.

At Pearl Harbor itself, there were incidents that, properly interpreted, might have given a brief warning. Four hours before the decisive moment, a Japanese submarine was sighted by the minesweeper USS Condor. About two and a half hours later, the commander of the destroyer USS Ward sent a message saying that he had attacked, fired upon, and dropped depth charges upon submarine operating in defensive sea area near Pearl Harbor. While Kimmel waited for confirmation of this report, the Japanese opened hostilities. In these same morning hours, U.S. Army Private George Elliott, practicing on the radar set after its normal closing time, noticed a large flight of planes on the screen. When he telephoned his lieutenant, he was told to disregard the observation, as a flight of B-17 bombers from the United States was expected at that time. Once again, an opportunity was missed.

The first Japanese dive-bomber appeared over Pearl Harbor at 7:55am (local time). It was part of a first wave of nearly 200 aircraft, including torpedo planes, bombers, and fighters. Within a quarter of an hour the various airfields at the base were subjected to savage attack. Due to Short's anti-sabotage measures, the U.S. military aircraft were packed tightly together at the Naval Air Station on Ford Island and adjoining Wheeler and Hickam fields, and many were destroyed on the ground by Japanese strafing. At Wheeler Field in particular the destruction was fearful. Of the 126 planes on the ground, 42 were destroyed, 41 were damaged, and only 43 were left fit for service. Only 6 U.S. planes got into the air to repel the attackers of this first assault. In total, more than 180 aircraft were destroyed.

surprise), they were not fully manned. Most of the damage to the battleships was inflicted in the first 30 minutes of the assault. The battleship USS Arizona blew up with an explosion. Riddled with bombs and torpedoes, the USS West Virginia settled on an even keel on the bottom of the harbour. The USS Oklahoma, hit by four torpedoes within five minutes, rolled completely over, with its bottom and propeller rising above the waters of the harbour. The USS California, the flagship of the Pacific Battle Force, was torpedoed and ordered abandoned as it slowly sank in shallow water. The target ship USS Utah also was sunk. Hardly a vessel escaped damage. The anti-aircraft crews on the various vessels were prompt in getting into action, and army personnel fired with what they had, but the force of the attack was in no serious way blunted.

At 8:50am the second wave of the attack began. Less successful than the first, it nonetheless inflicted heavy damage. The battleship USS Nevada had sustained a torpedo hit during the first wave, but its position at the end of Battleship Row allowed it greater freedom of action than the other moored ships. It was attempting to get underway when the second wave hit. It was struck by seven or eight bombs and was grounded at the head of the channel. The battleship USS Pennsylvania was set ablaze by bombs, and the two destroyers moored near it were reduced to wrecks. The destroyer USS Shaw was split in two by a great fireball and explosion. Shortly after 9:00am the Japanese withdrew.

No one could doubt that the Japanese had gained a great success. The Arizona and the Oklahoma were destroyed with great loss of life, and six other battleships suffered varying degrees of damage. Three cruisers, three destroyers, and other vessels were also damaged. U.S. military casualties totalled more than 3,400, including more than 2,300 killed. Heavy damage was inflicted on both army and navy aircraft on the ground. The Japanese lost up to 60 planes, five midget submarines, perhaps one or two fleet submarines, and fewer than 100 men. The Japanese task force retired from the theatre of battle without being attacked. Meanwhile in Europe in January 1942 U.S. troops arrive in Europe, all of them based across the UK

Through March, the number of troops shipped overseas averages about 50,000 per month -- a number that will soar upwards of 250,000 per month in 1944. In August Germany begins its assault on the Russian city of Stalingrad. In a battle that will rage on for six months and take hundreds of thousands of German and Russian lives, the Red Army finally defeats invading Nazis. The long, bloody battle proves to be a turning point in the war, as Germany began a retreat from the Eastern Front heading back to their theatres of war in France, Scandinavia the Low Countries, and North Africa.

In January 1943 Roosevelt and Churchill hold a conference in Casablanca, Morocco. They affirm their goal of securing the Axis nations' unconditional surrender. In May U.S. troops led by Generals Dwight D Eisenhower and George Patton join forces with British troops under the command of Field Marshal Bernard Montgomery to defeat German Field Marshal Erwin Rommel in North Africa. By the summer Dwight D Eisenhower was appointed commander of the U.S. forces in Europe. North Africa. By the summer Dwight D Eisenhower was appointed commander of the U.S. forces in Europe.

When the Allies won the North African Campaign on 13 May 1943, a quarter of a million German and Italian troops surrendered in Tunisia, on the north coast of Africa. With the huge Allied army and navy in the southern Mediterranean now freed for further action, British and American strategists faced two options: Transfer these forces north for the impending invasion of Europe from the English Channel, or remain in theatre to strike at southern Italy, which British Prime Minister Winston Churchill called "the soft underbelly of Europe." At this crossroads, the Allies, after some dissension, decided to press north into Italy. The stepping stone to its mainland would be the island of Sicily, in part because the Allies could depend on fighter cover from air bases on British Malta, 60 miles south of Sicily and recently freed from a siege by Axis forces. The invasion was assisted by some unique British subterfuge. In April 1943, a month before the Allied victory in North Africa, German agents recovered the body of a British Royal Marine pilot from the waters off a Spanish beach. Documents, in an attaché case handcuffed to the officer's wrist, provided a goldmine of intelligence about the Allies' secret plans, and German agents quickly sent the documents up the chain of command where they soon reached German Adolph Hitler who studied the captured plans carefully, and, taking full advantage of their top-secret details, directed his troops and ships to reinforce the islands of Sardinia and Corsica, west of Italy, against an impending Allied invasion. There was only one problem: The recovered body–which was not a Royal Marine but a homeless man from Wales, and its documents, were an elaborate British diversion called "Operation Mincemeat". (Two movies "The Man Who Never Was" (1956) and "Operation Mincemeat" (2022) faithfully tell this story). By the time Hitler redirected his troops in the summer of 1943, a massive Allied invasion force was sailing to Sicily.

The invasion of Sicily, code-named "Operation Husky", began before dawn on 10 July 1943, with combined air and sea landings involving 150,000 troops, 3,000 ships and 4,000 aircraft, all directed at the southern shores of the island. This massive assault was nearly cancelled the previous day when a summer storm arose and caused serious difficulties for paratroopers dropping behind enemy lines that night. However, the storm also worked to the Allies' advantage when Axis defenders along the Sicilian coast judged that no commander would attempt amphibious landings in such wind and rain. By the afternoon of 10 July 1943, supported by shattering naval and aerial bombardments of enemy positions, 150,000 Allied troops reached the Sicilian shores, bringing along 600 tanks. The landings progressed with Lieutenant General George S. Patton, commanding the American, and General Bernard L. Montgomery leading the British ground forces. Allied troops encountered light resistance to their combined operations. Hitler had been so deceived by "Mincemeat" that he had left only two German divisions in Sicily to battle Allied soldiers. Even several days into the attack he was convinced that it was a diversionary manoeuvre and continued to warn his officers to expect the main landings at Sardinia or Corsica. The Axis defence of Sicily was also weakened by losses the German and Italian armies had suffered in North Africa, in casualties as well as the several hundred thousand troops captured at the end of the campaign.

On 25 July, the day after Mussolini's arrest, the first Italian troops began withdrawing from Sicily. Hitler instructed his forces to make contingency plans for withdrawal but to continue to fight fiercely against the Allied advance. As July turned to August, Patton and Montgomery and their armies battled against determined German troops dug into the mountainous Sicilian terrain. The U.S. and British soldiers pushed back the Axis forces farther and farther until most were trapped in a northeast corner of the island.

As Patton and Montgomery closed in on the northeastern port of Messina, the German and Italian armies managed (over several nights) to evacuate 100,000 men, along with vehicles, supplies and ammunition, across the Strait of Messina to the Italian mainland. When his American soldiers moved into Messina on 17 August 1943, Patton, expecting to fight one final battle, was surprised to learn that the enemy forces had disappeared. The battle for Sicily was complete, but German losses had not been severe, and the Allies' failure to capture the fleeing Axis armies undermined their victory. The advance against the Italian mainland in September would take more time and cost the Allies more troops than they anticipated.

With so much going on, and little news filtering into German controlled Luxembourg, Anthony made the difficult decision to abandon his close-knit community of friends and lovers and disappear into the night without any goodbyes. That is how it appeared, but he hid away in an abandoned Alfa bedroom with all his chattels and sufficient food for a week. The bedroom chosen was towards the rear of the hotel, so that he could make his real "great escape" directly onto the railway station platform. He was able to study the movement of passenger and military services. Plus keep an eye on regular munitions movements by rail.

Apart from trains leaving for Amsterdam and German cities there seemed a dearth of services into France apart from heavily guarded "war-horses", so taking a train to Paris was not an option for our faux officer.

The choices were into Belgium and then cross into France and at the Petange or Esch-sur-Alzette. "Esch" was the country's leading production zone for the manufacture of high-quality steel. World

War II severely affected steel production, and many steel mills were either destroyed or heavily damaged. Luxembourg had been officially absorbed into Germany, and ARBED was temporarily renamed Hüttenwerke Burbach-Eich-Dudelingen (Burbach-Eich-Dudelange Metallurgical Plants). The company group used several hundred forced labourers and prisoners of war from the Soviet Union, France, Belgium, Poland, and Italy.

Anthony chose to cross into France at Esch-sur-Alzette and travel to Charleville on the River Meuse.

CHAPTER TEN: VIVE LA FRANCE – ON THE WAY

Luxembourg Resistance in Esch-sur-Alzette with liberated prisoners

Decked out in his German Officer finery, Oberleutnant Anton Heidelberg commandeered a pool military vehicle from a convoy of some twenty or so parked in the goods yard of the railway station and swiftly headed in the direction of Esch. He chose a The Volkswagen Type 82 Kübelwagen., Full-scale production of the Type 82 Kübelwagen started in February 1940, as soon as the VW factories had become operational. As of March 1943, the car received a more modern revised dash and the bigger 1,131 cc engine, developed for the Schwimmwagen, that produced more torque and power than the original 985 cc unit. When Volkswagen production ceased at the end of the war, 50,435 Kübelwagen vehicles had been made, and the vehicle had proven to be surprisingly useful, reliable, and durable, the British Army used them after the war.

In late 1943, apart from the occasional Zollgrenzschutz (customs Border Guards, an organization under the German Finance Ministry charged with guarding Germany's borders, acting as a combination Border Patrol and Customs & Immigration service) there were no checks on his 30 minute journey through south west

Luxembourg to Esch-sur-Alzette. At the border into France, it was staffed by elderly soldiers who just waved him through.

Obtaining fuel in France during WWII was a matter of coupons and contraband. From stolen military bowsers, the black market and bartering it was a tricky problem. Petrol was strictly rationed, and people received coupons that allowed them to purchase limited quantities. These coupons were essential for acquiring fuel for vehicles, and people had to use them wisely to ensure their vehicles remained operational. The French government carefully controlled the distribution of petrol through this coupon system. People found innovative ways to conserve petrol. Carpooling, using bicycles, or walking were encouraged to reduce fuel consumption, and some individuals modified their vehicles to run on alternative fuels or even used horse-drawn carts when possible. After the German occupation of France, the situation became more complex. The Germans controlled access to resources, including petrol. They prioritised their military needs. French citizens faced even stricter restrictions, and obtaining petrol became even more challenging.

Once outside of Luxembourg, Anthony decided to avoid going through Reims on his way to Paris and headed to the Champagne district using all the byroads to avoid any military convoys. During the Second World War, the wine producing area of Champagne remained outside of the battle zone. In June 1940 the German Army swept into France from the Aisne to the Seine and crossed the Marne without meeting serious resistance, despite the individual and collective heroism of many involved. Vitry-le-François was at the centre of the fighting during the first Battle of the Marne. Following the French victory, it became one of the conflict's most important relief centres. Located 60 km behind the front, this "hospital town" took in between 2,000 and 3,000 wounded, into ten medical facilities, during the major offensives, when the area was occupied by German forces for four tumultuous years. The initial siege resulted in the destruction of railway stations, and some villages, including Vitry-le-François, suffered heavy damage.

Retreating French soldiers, blew up some of their own bridges to slow the German advancement, but the town was burnt to the ground.

There was appalling destruction in Châlons-sur-Marne, and around the bridges that the French Army blew up as they retreated, and near the railway stations they were bombed by the German air force. Thankfully, the wine producing areas were spare,d and the vine growers and merchants generally did not experience too much damage. They took initiatives to hide much of their wine stocks behind fake walls in the deep chalky caves. As the war progressed, the vineyard upkeep and winemaking production once again was delegated to the women, children, and older men. Able-bodied surviving Frenchmen were either fighting in battlefields far away or had been taken to prison camps in Germany. Some wine was produced during the four-year period of German occupation, but not much. There were some very good vintages such as in 1943 but only in limited quantities. There was no chance that exports could be sent to any enemy of the Axis. There was a shortage of labourers, and there was no money to pay them or extra food rations to feed them.

The Germans encouraged production, so they could continue to be supplied with wine, and requestioned their "premier cru" calling the confiscation a levy. They eventually set up a system and paid the merchants to promote production, but they also continued to impose heavy taxes on sales. The Germans allowed the Champenois to sell surplus wine to the French and to neutral countries. Taxes were generally paid with bottles of champagne. An arrangement was established between the Champenois and the Germans that allowed business to continue in the area.

In 1941 the C.I.V.C. (Comite Interprofessionnel du Vin de Champagne) was formed to improve relations between growers and merchants and to help establish cooperation with the Germans. The organization is still in existence today and functions as a trade organization established by law to direct the common interests of merchants and growers. In 1943 the Resistance Movement became stronger in Champagne and the situation with the Germans began to deteriorate. The Germans arrested or deported several merchants, high ranking employees and growers along with high-ranking officials from France's regulatory agencies. Piper Heidsieck and Moet & Chandon were sequestered because of reported resistance activities. A feeling of hopelessness gripped the area. For four long years, Champagne was occupied by the Germans and, while its possessions were kept relatively safe, many of its men found themselves far away, in prison camps or taken over the Rhine as forced labour, or in free France or the French army in Algeria. Work was difficult in the vineyards. As well as the lack of labour there were chronic shortages of most things, including products to treat the vines and horses. Vine growers used oxen, as was the custom in the Médoc. During the harvests it was hard to find enough pickers, and even if they could be found, there was only a diet of thick-skinned wine grapes to eat – not even bread!

Sales to the countries at war with the Axis were, of course, impossible and in 1941 the press signalled the return to the United States of the bootleggers offering champagne substitutes as well as authentic champagne, just as in the heyday of Prohibition.

The production of champagne did, however, continue, not only because of its importance to the region's economy but also because the Germans required a supply for their army and to use as currency in their exchanges with neutral countries.

On their arrival in Champagne, they carried out what Maurice Hollande referred to as, using a charitable euphemism, prélèvements incontrôlés ("uncontrolled levies") which resulted in the disappearance from the merchants' cellars of more than two million bottles, and that does not, of course, include the thousands of bottles that were left in their personal cellars by inhabitants who fled before the invasion

Sales to the countries at war with the Axis were, of course, impossible and in 1941 the press signalled the return to the United States of the bootleggers offering champagne substitutes as well as authentic champagne, just as in the heyday of Prohibition. The production of champagne did, however, continue, not only because of its importance to the region's economy but also because the Germans required a supply for their army and to use as currency in their exchanges with neutral countries. On their arrival in Champagne, they carried out what Maurice Hollande referred to as, using a charitable euphemism, prélèvements incontrôlés ("uncontrolled levies") which resulted in the disappearance from the merchants' cellars of more than two million bottles, and that does not, of course, include the thousands of bottles that were left in their personal cellars by nicknamed the champagne führer by the inhabitants of Champagne. The levies continued, varying annually until the end of the war from between 15 and 18 million bottles, but these were carried out in an orderly fashion; the merchants were paid, and they were free to sell the surplus in France and to the neutral countries. Inhabitants who fled before the invasion. The occupation authorities soon established an office in Rheims charged with the coordination of German purchases and the fixing of levies. It was run by a certain Otto Klaebisch, who was immediately nicknamed the champagne führer by the inhabitants of Champagne.

The levies continued, varying annually until the end of the war from between 15 and 18 million bottles, but these were carried out in an orderly fashion; the merchants were paid, and they were free to sell the surplus in France and to the neutral countries.

Fortunately, nature was generous. Apart from 1940, when there were so many disasters that the harvest was lost, the drought of the following four years has made mildew a certainty (translator's note: mildew was not always undesirable) and enabled huge economies in copper sulphate.

oïdium, after being aggressive in 1943, has been benign during the other years.

There has been no grape moth, little or no harvest worms, just one frost in the spring, but more in 1944 so there was some good wine every year and even, in 1943, an exceptional wine which will be talked about for years to come, as were the local "Jerry-Bags" who more than fraternised with their Nazi lovers.

A certain agreement was thus established between the occupied and the occupiers, but at the end of 1943 the situation deteriorated because the Resistance movement started to become active in Champagne. The Germans hardened their attitude towards Resistance activities. Having been tipped off that an organisation existed within Moët & Chandon, they arrested those in charge; Paul Chandon-Moët was deported to Auschwitz and Robert-Jean de Vogüé, who was condemned to death and incarcerated in a fortress, narrowly escaped execution.

They also arrested Claude Fourmon, the director of the Comité Interprofessionnel du Vin de Champagne (see below), who was sent to Buchenwald, and then to Dora. The repression continued. Numerous merchants and vine growers were deported; amongst them Bertrand de Vogüé, the brother of Robert-Jean and president-director-general of Vve Clicquot Ponsardin, and Gaston Poittevin, the president of the Syndicat Général des Vignerons, who were deported to Neuengamme and Buchenwald respectively. Some champagne houses were put under sequestration, notably Moët and Chandon, for the reasons indicated above, and Piper-Heidsieck, when the good old English Army parachutes were discovered in their cellars. To summarise the camouflage of protection by the German Occupation of the areas was more than a double-edged sword.

From merciless pillaging to despotic administration, perhaps no winegrowing region suffered more frustrations during World War II than Champagne. But is it not strange how the seemingly worst occasions in a region's (or nation's) history almost always wind up leading to moments of triumph? A finest hour? For the Champenois, the challenges faced under Nazi occupation were precisely this: a five-year period of unprecedented beleaguerment, yet one positively inundated with instances of resourcefulness and selflessness.

Following the surrender of France on 22 June 1940, the major winegrowing regions of the nation were placed under charge of the 'weinführer,' each with a mandate to supply the Third Reich with copious quantities of wine. In Champagne, the man appointed for this task was Otto Klaebisch. Born in Cognac and belonging to the family firm of Matteüs-Müller, the Champenois were relieved to learn that their overseer had actually been involved in the wine (initially brandy) trade. In the words of one producer: 'If you were going to be shoved around, it was better to be shoved around by a winemaker than by some beer-drinking Nazi lout.' Such sentiments proved short-lived. Unlike other weinführer stationed throughout France, Herr Klaebisch seemed to truly enjoy the accoutrements of military life, almost always wearing his uniform when conducting affairs. He was also callously greedy. After a fleeting glance at the château of Veuve Clicquot-Ponsardin, he sent owner Bertrand de Vogüé and his family packing.

Herr Klaebisch poured a glass for them both, asking his guest what he thought of the wine. Before Hodez could reply, the former made his thoughts clear: 'Let me tell you what I think. It smells like shit! And this is what you want me to give the Wehrmacht to drink?' Hodez was subsequently thrown out of the office.On another occasion, 20-year-old François Taittinger was summoned to appear before Klaebisch, who was upset that the young man's firm had submitted demonstrably inferior bottlings. 'How dare you send us fizzy dishwater!' he exclaimed. Taittinger's retort: 'Who cares? It's not as if it's going to be drunk by people who know anything about Champagne!' The weinführer immediately threw him in jail, albeit for just a few days until François' eldest brother Guy could secure his release. To handle such volatility, creative diplomacy proved a much better approach. At Bollinger, 'Madame Jacques' devised her own means of keeping Herr Klaebisch (at least directly) out of the way. Receiving the man with courtesy and dignity, she offered him an armchair so narrow that it was unable to accommodate his considerable girth, compelling Herr Klaebisch to continually stand throughout his visit. For the rest of the occupation, he never called on Bollinger again, and the chair remains at the house today. This incident aside, there was unquestionably no person better able to handle Herr Klaebisch than Count Robert-Jean de Vogüé. As head of Moët & Chandon, and a man with extensive family links to some of Europe's most powerful families, de Vogüé was just about the only person to whom the weinführer ever displayed any deference.

Until de Vogüé's (pictured third from the left) arrest in 1943, the two men had many meetings. For their part, the other major houses entrusted de Vogüé with securing as many concessions as possible. And while de Vogüé's victories were few and far between, there is no doubt his efforts prevented the Champenois from becoming considerably worse off during the occupation. One such effort was the creation of the Comité Interprofessionnel du Vin de Champagne (CIVC). By ordered (among other things) to dispatch enormous quantities of the celebrated 1928 vintage to Berlin every month. Then-president Christian de Billy noted: 'We never had a lot of it and tried to hide what we could, but it was so wonderful and so well known that it was impossible to keep it out of German hands. Klaebisch knew it was there.'

The response of the Champenois was one of unprecedented unison. On 10 April 1941, de Vogüé called together producers and growers to set up an organisation that would represent the interests of everyone in the Champagne industry. 'We are all in this together,' he stated. 'We will either suffer or survive but we will do so equally.' Three days later, the CIVC was established, and has continued to function as the representative body of the region to this very day. That said, at the time of its founding the objective of the CIVC was a tad more simplistic: to enable producers to present a united front to the occupiers and speak with a single voice. Not surprisingly, de Vogüé was appointed its top representative. Although Herr Klaebisch was unhappy about the creation of this new organisation, he was compelled to do business with its members. He outlined his position to de Vogüé in a rather acrimonious meeting: 'You can sell to the Third Reich and its military, and also to German controlled restaurants, hotels and nightclubs, and a few of our friends like the Italian ambassador to France and Marshal Pétain at Vichy.' When informed of just how much Champagne was expected to be delivered each month, de Vogüé asked the weinführer how the CIVC could possibly carry this out. His opponent's boisterous response: 'Work Sundays!' Although the two men eventually came to a compromise, such an episode illustrates the nature of their relationship, as both seemed to understand just how far the other could be pushed. To an extent, the CIVC was reasonably successful in defending its interests against Herr Klaebisch and his enforcement officers. Eventually, it was even granted permission to sell a quarter of its annual production to civilians in France, Belgium, Sweden and Finland. The CIVC was also able to keep most firms running by rotating experienced workers from one Champagne house to another. Through such cooperation, most establishments could endure.

However, it is important to remember that the CIVC was not the only organisation working hard making peoples' lives better. Throughout the occupation of France, the Resistance was extremely busy in Marne using vineyard transport to fight the Boche. Early on, freedom fighters had become aware of the fact that major Champagne shipments to a specific part of Europe or Africa tended to precede a significant military offensive. A notable example of this occurred in late-1941, when an enormous order included the unusual request that bottles be specially corked and packed so that they could be sent to 'a very hot country'. That country turned out to be Egypt, where General Rommel was about to begin his North African campaign. The Resistance passed along this information to British intelligence in London. In such ways, the Champenois successfully survived the occupation of World War II, confounding the weinführer at almost every turn in a widespread, selfless campaign to protect that which mattered most. Not long before Champagne's liberation, Herr Klaebisch was recalled to Germany, leaving behind millions of francs' worth of unpaid bills and a wounded pride from which he likely never fully recovered. This was a pathetic and wholly anticlimactic conclusion for the weinführer of Champagne.

It had been a sensible diversion for Anthony to conceal his German Army vehicle, change his clothes and become a drifting worker trying to get work as a labourer in the Champagne cellars for a few weeks. The only visible German transport was destined to Paris packed with crates of posh fizz, together with a ramshackle group of German Soldiers posted in and around the producers' caves, with little else to do but barter with the local market traders.After a month of working cash-in-hand loading up German Military transport with crates of fizz, it was time for Anthony to become Oberleutnant Anton Heidelberg once again. This time when retrieving his Volkswagen Type 82 Kübelwagen he followed the booze convoy to Paris under the protection of a safely in numbers cavalcade providing the resistance were not about to ambush.

For those in Europe it was easy to forget that in December 1943 World War II was truly of global proportions. The occupation of much of Europe was still under the Jackboot. (These boots were associated with Fascism, particularly the German Nazi soldiers, as they were initially worn by members of the Sturmabteilung and later the field forces of the Wehrmacht and Waffen-SS as part of the World War II German uniform before and even after Germany experienced leather shortages. When goose-stepping on pavement, the large columns of German soldiers in Marschstiefel - "marching boots" created a distinct bone-crunching sound which came to symbolise German conquest and occupation.)

CHAPTER ELEVEN: AN OWN DE GAULLE

After the "Phoney War," the calm period between the invasion of Poland and May 1940, the Nazis swooped on France, deftly invading and defeating the country within seven weeks. When they arrived in the capital on 14 June, the victors wasted no time in laying claim to the city's world-famous avenue. A military parade and marching bands descended on Les Champs-Elysées, hanging a swastika flag from the Arc de Triomphe. Two weeks later, Hitler proudly promenaded down the avenue on his grand tour of Paris, his only wartime visit there, and was visibly smug.

Most of the resistance by ordinary Parisians was symbolic: encouraged by the BBC, students scribbled the letter V for *Victory* on walls, blackboards, tables, and on the side of cars. The Germans tried to co-opt the 'V' campaign, placing huge Vs. symbolizing their own victories, on the Eiffel Tower and the National Assembly, but with little effect. During the German invasion of May 1940, General De Gaulle led an armoured division which counterattacked the invaders; he was then appointed under-secretary for War. Refusing to accept his government's armistice with Germany, De Gaulle fled to England and exhorted the French to continue the fight. For many Frenchmen his vanishing act to London was a betrayal, especially for the people of Paris, and his claim that he was leading the Free French Forces in absentia was fraudulent leaving behind "his" loyal resistance fighters to be supported by a network of British agents; men and women who risked and often gave their lives to free France from their Nazi tyranny. De Gaulle at Broadcasting House insisted that there would not be any reference to the BBC. He was on-air claiming to be from Radio Londres.

**De Gaulle at Broadcasting House insisting that the
BBC logo be removed from his microphone.**

From the signing of the Molotov–Ribbentrop Pact in August 1939, until June 1941, the Communists played no active part in the Resistance. The Vichy government and Germans allowed their newspapers to publish, and they made no mention of the patriotic demonstrations on 11 November. But after Operation Barbarossa, the German attack on the Soviet Union on 22 June 1941, the communists became the most active and best-organised forces against the Germans. They remained hostile to de Gaulle, whom reactionary British puppet. On 21 August 1941, a 21-year-old veteran communist named Pierre Georges, who used the clandestine name "Fabien", shot the German naval officer Alfons Moser, in the back, as he was boarding the Metro at the Barbés-Rochecouart station. The Germans had routinely taken hostages among the French civilian population to deter attacks. They responded to the Barbés-Rochechouart metro attack by executing three hostages in Paris, and another twenty the following month. Hitler was furious at the leniency of the German commander, and demanded that in case of future assassinations, there must be one hundred hostages executed for every German killed. After the next killing of a German, forty-eight hostages were immediately shot by firing squad. From London, General de Gaulle condemned the Communist policy of random assassinations, saying the cost in innocent civilian lives was too high, and it had no impact on the war but the random shooting of Germans continued. In retaliation, an estimated 1,400 hostages from the Paris region were taken and 981 executed by the German military at Fort Mont Valérien.

Acts of resistance in Paris became more dangerous. In the spring of 1942, five students of the Lycée Buffon decided to protest the arrest of one of their teachers. About one hundred students took part, chanting the teacher's name and throwing leaflets. The demonstrators escaped, but the police tracked down and arrested the five student leaders, who were tried and executed on 8 February 1943.

As the war continued, resistance forces were divided largely between the groups; followers of General de Gaulle in London, and those organised by the Communists. Thanks to pressure from the British, who supplied the weapons, and the diplomacy of one Resistance leader, Jean Moulin, who created the National Council of the Resistance (Conseil National de la Resistance CNR), the different factions began to coordinate.

Many of Paris's luxury hotels were requisitioned by the Nazis, and the elegant Le Meurice (pictured above) opposite the Tuileries Garden, between Place de la Concorde and the Musée du Louvre on the Rue de Rivoli was repurposed into the headquarters of the German occupation of "Gross Paris" (greater Paris). During 1944, as the war's endgame was beginning, a new military governor of Paris, General Dietrich von Choltitz, moved in. Specifically chosen for his track record of rigid obedience, he was on strict instruction from Hitler to destroy the city rather than let it fall into the hands of the Allies. However, a few weeks later, the famous question Hitler asked von Choltitz, "IS PARIS BURNING?", would not receive an affirmative answer. The story (which is disputed) goes that during meetings at Le Meurice, the Swedish consul-general in Paris, Raoul Nordling, helped convince von Choltitz to defy the Fuhrer's orders and spare Paris. No matter what transpired at that meeting, the hotel was stormed by the French Free Forces, to whom von Choltitz surrendered—a bullet hole next to the "M" above the main door is a more definite testament to that event.

It was into this hotel (pictured above) on 4 December 1943, festooned with Christmas decorations, that Anthony, resplendent in his Oberleutnant Anton Heidelberg garb checked in. Being under the remit of the Germany military within the confines of Le Meurice he was able to use his Reichsmarks but how would he move around Paris without domestic currency?

Monsieur Bernard Martin de Concierge was the unauthorised Bureau de Change – he? Was he a collaborator? Was he working for the resistance, and how could Anton test his loyalties and what would buy his silence? The three evils of society were always the paymaster. Sex, drugs, and "pieces d'or", and Oberleutnant Anton Heidelberg could supply all three. Le Pièces d'Or were Swedish Crowns and British Sovereigns, the Drugs – German Pervatin; and as for sex Anthony could easily buy the services of a handful of Prostituées Parisiennes. His first move was to ask Monsieur Martin to procure a hooker in a most discrete manner asking Bernard what was his choice of debauchery? Did he have any special fetishes himself that he might be willing to "share"? It worked – Martin was bursting with excitement at the possibility of an erotic experience paid for by a member of what he believed to be the occupying force. During the World War II German occupation of France, 20 top Paris brothels, including Le Chabanais, Le Sphinx, One-Two-Two, La Fleur Blanche, and the naughty Chez Marguerite.

These were mostly reserved by the Wehrmacht for German officers and collaborating Frenchmen. These brothels flourished and Hermann Göring visited Le Chabanais. Monsieur Martin confessed that he had never been into any brothel but received commissions from brothel owners for recommending their establishments. He suggested that the kinkiest establishment famous for its torture room was Las Fleur Blanche on La Rue des Moulins. La Fleur blanche was notably frequented by artist Toulouse-Lautrec, where he painted over 40 prostitutes there in the

1890s. A call by Martin to the madame and the Oberleutnant was on the way after being advised that German Marks would be acceptable.

The anonymous street entrance gave way to a cornucopia of 19th century artistic splendour mixed with an aurora sensual lighting and decadence. A posh pink pouting paradise parlour of provocative persuasions with perfumes permeating from the perfectly posed, pretty prostitutes.

Those girls with regular German Officer clients cultivated their relationships and were who in turn passed on their reports to Britain's Special Operations Executive. The girls would also assist in helping deserters, RAF airmen and Jews in hiding.

The Special Operations Executive (SOE) was the leading World War II organisation dedicated to espionage, sabotage, and reconnaissance missions in occupied Europe. Highly dangerous, the agents of the SOE risked their lives daily in the interest of driving the Nazis out of Allied territory and bringing an end to the war.

Vichy asked women to do nothing less than to save the soul of France by building families. In addition, or instead, they helped men escape, hid Jews, and joined the resistance. They also lived their everyday lives, staining their legs with iodine when they couldn't afford stockings. "Our role was to put on the costume," wrote the actor Corinne Luchaire, who was later sentenced to 10 years of dégradation nationale for "collaboration horizontale".

Without their clothes on these girls were fighting for survival whilst at the same time fighting for a Free France. Wearing their para-military clothing supplied by the British SOE, they were resistance fighters, and proud to be so. By sleeping with the enemy, they had the advantage of knowing more of what was in the planning stages. It was accepted that before WWII one-in-five young men in Paris society were encouraged by their fathers to experience sex for the first time by losing their virginity to a prostitute.

Il faut apprendre à baiser, et la meilleure prof est une prostituée.

The curvy creatures working their crafts within the Chabanais were not your normal street girls. They were in the main highly educated multi-lingual collectors of information necessary to Allied government operatives, dressed in fatigues when "off duty" which were supplied by the British, and trained in all manners of espionage by their SOE contacts. Several of the girls were morse proficient and were often asked to be SOE radio operators (Pictured below).

In June 1940, Winston Churchill appointed Hugh Dalton at the head of a new and highly secretive organisation – the SOE. Intended to combat the terrifying progress of Adolf Hitler's army into France, Churchill gave Dalton a bold order: 'Set Europe ablaze.' The SOE set about training a team of secret agents to be sent undercover into Nazi-occupied France. Among these were 41 women, who fearlessly endured all manner of terrors to perform their wartime duties.

The SOE F Section was particularly hazardous: it involved working directly from Nazi-occupied France, sending information back to the Allies, aiding the Resistance movement, and hindering the German campaign in any way possible. Despite the clear risks, SOE agents had to be faultlessly confident in their abilities, as SOE courier Francine Agazarian once commented: "I believe none of us in the field ever gave one thought to danger. Germans were everywhere, especially in Paris; one absorbed the sight of them and went on with the job of living as ordinarily as possible. An SOE agent had to appear to know everyone whilst at the same time becoming invisible in a crowd. Caution when walking the streets was paramount, with "twenty-twenty vision" to avoid domestic confrontation, fights, arrests or roundups was imperative to survive.

Though all working for the United Kingdom, the women of the SOE F Section hailed from across the globe. They all had one thing in common however: the ability to speak French, as assimilation into their surroundings was vital for the success of missions knowing that every day, every hour and every minute, death was around every corner.

These SOE operatives were subjected to terrible interrogation not from the Germans but from members of the French resistance fighters." La Résistance" was a collection of groups that fought the Nazi occupation of France and the collaborationist Vichy régime in France during the Second World War. Resistance cells were small groups of armed men and women (called the Maquis in rural areas) who conducted guerrilla warfare and published underground newspapers. They also provided first-hand intelligence information, and escape networks that helped Allied soldiers and airmen trapped behind Axis lines.

These SOE operatives were subjected to terrible interrogation not from the Germans but from members of the French resistance fighters." La Résistance" was a collection of groups that fought the Nazi occupation of France and the collaborationist Vichy régime in France during the Second World War.

Resistance cells were small groups of armed men and women (called the Maquis in rural areas) who conducted guerrilla warfare and published underground newspapers. They also provided first-hand intelligence information, and escape networks that helped Allied soldiers and airmen trapped behind Axis lines.

The Resistance's men and women came from many parts of French society, including émigrés, school teachers, doctors, nurses and academics.

Catholics, Protestants, Jews, Muslims, Liberals, Anarchists, Com munists, prostitutes and even disillusioned fascists. The proportion of French people who participated in organised resistance has been estimated at from one to three percent of the total population.

Although suspicious of the British female agents, without their help and support from the SOE, they would not have enjoyed the technical strategic command or the supplies of arms and money from Whitehall.

From 19-year-old Sonya Butt from Kent in England to 53-year-old Marie-Thérèse Le Chêne from Sedan in France, the women of the SOE encompassed a variety of ages and backgrounds. As the secretive organisation could not openly recruit its members, they instead had to rely on word of mouth, and as such many of the women of the SOE had relatives working alongside them, particularly brothers and husbands. On missions into France, the agents were either parachuted, flown, or taken by boat to their positions. From there, they were placed was apparently the 'best shot' the service had ever seen during her training and was soon sent to Indre Department in France as a courier.in teams of three, consisting of an 'organiser' or leader, wireless operator and courier. Couriers were the first roles opened to women in the SOE, as they were able to travel more easily than men, who were often treated with suspicion. Almost all organisers within the different SOE networks were men, however one woman was able to rise to this position: Pearl Witherington. Joining the SOE in 1943, Witherington

was apparently the 'best shot' the service had ever seen during her training and was soon sent to Indre Department in France as a courier.

On 1 May 1944, a twist of fate saw Pearl's own organiser Maurice Southgate arrested by the Gestapo and taken to Buchenwald Concentration Camp, while she and her wireless operator Amédéé Maingard took the afternoon off. With Southgate a prisoner of the Germans, Pearl became the leader of her own SOE network, and together with Maingard at the helm of another, the pair caused over 800 interruptions of railway lines, hindering the German effort to transport troops and material to the battlefront in Normandy. The following month she narrowly escaped capture when 56 truckloads of German soldiers attacked her headquarters in the village of Dun-le-Poëlier, forcing her to flee into a nearby wheat field. The Germans did not pursue her however and instead focused on destroying the weapons found inside the building.

A key player in organising the French Maquis, or resistance fighters, four groups from Witherington's network were called upon to face an army of 19,000 German soldiers at the Forest of Gatine in August 1944. The Maquis threatened the Germans to the point of surrender, yet unwilling surrender to a group who weren't a 'regular army', they instead negotiated with US General Robert C Macon. To her fury, neither Witherington nor her maquis were invited to attend or participate in the official surrender. With her mission complete she returned to the UK in September 1944.

The SOE conceived the Welbike to create a small transportable vehicle for agents to use behind enemy lines. These bikes were disassembled and put into parachutable containers. Upon completion of the drop, agents could assemble the bike, which took about 11 seconds.

Lise de Baissac was recruited as a courier to the SOE in 1942, and alongside Andree Borrel was the first female agent to be parachuted into France. She then travelled to Poitiers to begin a solo mission spying on the Gestapo headquarters, living there for 11 months. Adopting the role of an amateur archaeologist, she cycled around the country identifying possible parachute drop-zones and landing areas, collecting air-dropped weapons and supplies for transport to safe houses, and building a resistance network of her own in the process. Her duties as a courier also involved receiving and briefing 13 newly arrived SOE agents and arranging the clandestine departure of agents and resistance leaders back to England. In essence, she and her fellow couriers were the key figures on the ground in France, carrying messages, receiving supplies, and aiding with local resistance movements. Her second mission into France was even more vital in 1943 when she was stationed in Normandy, unknowingly preparing for the D-Day landings. When she at last caught wind that the Allied invasion of France was imminent, she cycled 300km in three days to get back to her network, suffering many close calls with German officials. On one such occasion, she described how a group of Germans came to evict her from her accommodation, stating: "I arrived to take my clothes and found they had opened the parachute I had made into a sleeping bag and were sitting on it. Fortunately, they had no idea what it was."

Noor Inayat Khan was the first female wireless operator sent from the UK into occupied France. Of Indian Muslim and American heritage, Khan was university educated and an excellent musician – a skill that made her a naturally talented signaller. Acting as a wireless operator was perhaps the most dangerous role in the SOE. It involved maintaining the link between London and the resistance in France, sending messages back and forth at a time where detection by the enemy was improving as the war progressed. By 1943, the life expectancy of a wireless operator was just 6 weeks.

In June 1943, while many in her network were being gradually rounded up by the Germans, Khan opted to stay in France, believing herself to be the only SOE operator still in Paris. Soon after, she was betrayed by someone in the SOE's circle and underwent a harsh interrogation process by the Gestapo. She refused to give them any information, however after discovering her notebooks, the Germans were able to imitate her messages and communicate directly to London, facilitating the capture of a further three SOE agents. After a failed escape attempt, she was transported to Dachau Concentration Camp alongside her fellow female agents: Yolande Beekman, Madeleine Damerment and Eliane Plewman. All four were executed at dawn on 13 September 1944, with Khan's last word reported to be simply: "Liberté". Just under half of the 41 women recruited into the SOE did not survive the war. 12 were executed by the Nazis, two died of disease, one died on a sinking ship, and another died of natural causes. Out of the 41 agents, 17 saw the horrors inside the German concentration camps of Bergen-Belsen, Ravensbrück, and Dachau, including SOE survivor Odette Sansom whose story was captured in the 1950 film "Odette". 25 did make it home however and went on to live long and happy lives. Francine Agazarian lived to be 85, Lise de Baissac to 98, and Pearl Witherington to 93.The last living female SOE member was Phyllis Latour, who during her time as an agent sent over 135 coded messages from Normandy to Britain, knitted into her silken hair ties. In April 2021, she turned 100 years old and died 7 October 2023 (aged 102).

Oberleutnant Anton Heidelberg had to identify one Chabanais prostitute (above) from Forces Françaises de l'Intérieur, and to do that dressed as a German officer wasn't going to be easy. It would take a great deal of convincing a young girl that not only was he not a German Officer, but a British soldier "on the run". Anton told Madame Claude he was looking on behalf of Bernard Martin for a Luxembourg girl as the hotelier had a passion for something "foreign." He was introduced to Claire from Wiltz, a town 35 miles northwest of Luxembourg City. He paid the Madame 50 German Marks equivalent to 1,000 French Francs and a similar amount to the Luxembourg girl – a huge amount of money, but the patron was not about to complain. The two disappeared into one of the themed boudoirs where during some fornication Anthony was able to explain his situation and talk about who he really was, who he met and knew from her own country. Anthony had taken risks on a couple of occasions by owning up to who he really was and how he escaped from a German POW camp in Poland. Was Claire a Nazi informer? She cried, held him tight and pleaded for his help too. She had been trafficked out of Luxembourg, along with half a dozen other pretty girls as retribution following the General Strike, taken to Paris to become sex workers in the city's premiere brothels including the Chabanais.

On 30 August 1942, it was announced that all Luxembourger males of military age were to be conscripted into the Wehrmacht to fight against Allies. It was this decision that motivated the people of Luxembourg from anger to action, sticking to their national motto, "Mir woelle bleiwe waat mir sinn" (We want to remain what we are).

The Luxembourg population responded quickly against the forced conscription. Within hours citizens began organizing a general strike. On 31 August the strike officially began in the town of Wiltz. Local town officials, Michel Worré and Nicolas Müller, gathered other officials and refused to go to work. Slowly they were joined by other workers as the movement spread. Leaflets were printed by Anthony and distributed secretly throughout the country.

Soon after the striking in Wiltz, workers from the southwestern industrial towns of Schifflange and Differdange were alerted and refused to go to work. The strike spread also to the mining and steel manufacturing town Esch-sur-Alzette. Here, all aspects of the economic life were paralysed, including administration, agriculture, industry, and education structures.

The central Post Office in Luxembourg received formal confirmation of the strike soon after. Few mailbags were even opened as a mere semblance of work continued. At the approach of any German employee, the postal workers dispersed back to their workplaces and pretended to work. Only letters and packages clearly addressed to Luxembourgers who had been deported to Germany for forced labour, were handled with care. News in Allied countries began covering the protest as the first general strike to be held in a German-occupied territory. For the rest of the world, it exposed German propaganda, which claimed that the people of Luxembourg were voluntarily joining German forces.

Whole families were deported to East Germany on trains from Luxembourg's railway station (Luxembourgish: Gare Lëtzebuerg, French: Gare de Luxembourg, German: Bahnhof Luxemburg) , and replaced by German families who occupied their homes.

Of the Luxembourg men drafted for service in the German Wehrmacht, about 40% refused and went into hiding, half of them within the country's borders. Some escaped to Britain and joined the Allied forces to fight against Germany and the Axis powers. After the 1942 general strike, German occupation continued to repress the Luxembourger people. Thousands were arrested and tortured and hundreds died in concentration camps. Children were forced to work in the coal mines. German authorities, alert to any sign of resistance and fearing further escalation of protests, mobilized immediately. An order declaring a state of emergency and martial law was instigated with warnings that strikers were to be immediately shot.

Beginning 1 September 1943, German officials began arresting strike leaders. Within days, 21 leaders, many of whom were teachers, were arrested for interrogation and then executed. Michel Worré and Nicolas Müller, from Wiltz were tried by a military tribunal, sentenced to death, and deported to the Hinzert concentration camp in Germany just 19 miles from the Luxembourg border where they were shot.

According to a German officer who witnessed the executions of Worré and Müller, their lasts words were, "Vive Lëtzebuerg" (Long live Luxembourg!). Others were decapitated in the street. Many of the leaders' families were sent to prison and work camps in Germany. Following summary executions, the strike was effectively halted.

A series of posters were later posted throughout Luxembourg announcing the death of the strikers because of the strike, bearing the names, occupation, and residency of each victim. Although the exact number of strikers is unknown, the movement did mark Luxembourg's resistance to the German occupation, gaining attention worldwide.

Claire admitted to Anthony that being deported to Paris as a sex worker left her with a feeling of guilt, not because she was a prostitute, but having escaped from the barbaric occupation of her country by the Nazis. Having sex became routine and mostly was enjoyable with her regular clients who arrived not only with money for her services, but gifts of contraband luxury items. (I knew what it was like to have sex. I was sleeping with my teacher in Luxembourg from the age of 13 perhaps even 12). I would never meet my German lovers outside of the confines of the Chabanais fearing physical retribution from Parisians They were not expected to know that we were also working for the resistance fighters and the British SOE spy network, passing on "between the sheets" chatter about troop movements.

"I will not go to Le Meurice, two of my clients are billeted in that hotel, and you must not develop any procurement from this establishment for that concierge guy. He is dangerous. Give him some drugs and ask the madam here to give you a contact with a local dirty whore that will visit him. Hopefully she gifts him a bad case of gonorrhoea".

"I guess you want to get out of France and back home to England. Anthony, I want you to leave that hotel, and I will help you find a safe house. I also want you to take me with you, not to England, but to Panasqueira."

Anthony replied, "Where is Panasqueira, and why there?"

"My Uncle Damien lives there, and it is in Portugal. He was sent there in 1935 by his bosses the steel manufacturer ARBED S.A.,

(Aciéries Réunies de Burbach-Eich-Dudelange) which at the time was Europe's biggest and companies. He is a metallurgist, and Panasqueira is the world's biggest tungsten supplier."

(In 1911 the Wolfram Mining and Smelting Company was formed and purchased all the rights to the concessions including the buildings, the equipment and 125 hectares of rural land. In 1912, the new company made major investments in machinery and equipment, upgrading the Rio treatment plant, and installing the first aerial 5,100m rope-tramway that brought the ore from different mining sites at Panasqueira to the Rio plant. In 1912, the production of wolframite concentrates was reportedly 267 tons of 65% WO_3 (tungsten trioxide) mined by 244 workers from 10,791 tonnes of vein as well as 86,063 tonnes of host rock.)

Manpower increased from 750 workers in 1933 to 3,300 in 1940 and nearly 5,800 in 1943. Portugal was neutral during the war and the mine could count on a steady supply of workers and sales to both sides in the conflict. In addition, there were approximately 4,800 individual miners working the small veins on the surrounding hills.)

"From Panasqueira, my uncle sends Britain the best quality Tungsten. He tests and buys the metal and ships it out of the port Porto which is two hours away from the mines. I'm sure he would get you back to Britain with the tungsten."

Germany was particularly dependent on tungsten, which was essential for its war industry. The loss of key tungsten sources in Portugal and Spain early in the war led to the "Wolfram Crisis" that threatened Germany's ability to produce armoured vehicles and anti-tank munitions. Germany was forced to seek alternative sources in South America, Africa, and Asia. This scarcity shaped strategic decisions and influenced Germany's military capabilities and production capacity. Tungsten's usefulness extended beyond armour and projectiles. It was utilized for electrical contacts and filaments, strengthening steel alloys in aircraft, and in various tools and dies. Tungsten carbide's hardness made it ideal for machine tools and armour-piercing cores. The United States and Britain also relied on tungsten supplies from Asia and South America to satisfy wartime demand, but the quality paled into insignificance to that which emanated out of Portugal. In many ways, tungsten helped determine the course and outcome of armoured warfare during World War II. Its unique properties allowed it to armour vehicles while also defeating that same armour. Whichever nation could obtain adequate tungsten supplies enjoyed a strategic advantage. Tungsten truly was the unsung hero that helped tip the scales of victory and defeat.

Anthony dressed up again as Oberleutnant Anton Heidelberg promised Caire he would make an appointment with Madame Claude to see her again in a couple of days. The Madame was most delighted to open her diary to "book-in" the dapper, big spending Oberleutnant for a second visit. She also offered to arrange that Bernard Martin would get a call-girl call from the most fetish experienced whore in town, for which he gave her another 50 Reichmark note. He returned to Martin with the news to expect a telephone call from a pre-paid tart then discretely palming him with three "dont take them all at once" Pevitin pills, and a gold Swedish Crown. Sex, drugs and solid gold – signed, sealed and delivered.

Anthony returned to his room excited at the prospect that he was soon to be leaving Paris with an attractive popsie in the direction Panasqueira in Portugal. An early dinner of wild boar. (Wilde Sau, known in English as "Wild Boar" was the term given by the Luftwaffe to the tactic used from 1943 to 1944 during World War II by which British night bombers were engaged by single-seat day-fighter aircraft flying in the Defence of the Reich.)

How would he leave Paris? Should he dress as an Oberleutnant, or in civvies? "I will need a béret" he thought, "but a well-worn one, not a new one, though I doubt that there would be any new ones in the shops".

Surprisingly, rather than the French claiming all credit for inventing the beret, people tend to reference Noah (from the Bible) with the earliest ideas.

Legend has it that when Noah was bobbing around on his ark with all his animals, and getting soaked, he noticed that the trampled wool on the floor in the sheep pen had transformed into something we now call felt. Apparently, he cut out a circle, shoved it on his head to keep his hair dry, and the first ever beret was born.

CHAPTER TWELVE

ANTHONY'S MAQUIS INTERROGATION

It was time for Anthony to have his second faux sexual encounter as Oberleutnant Anton Heidelberg with Claire. He paid Madame his usual fee, and she smiled saying "At this time your Monsieur Martin will be having his erotic wishes granted."

Claire was ecstatic to see Anthony. You are to leave your hotel early tomorrow morning dressed as you are now and take all your belongings with you. Pick me up outside of Chabanais at 6.00am – we are driving to a safe house in Poitiers. I will warn you now that it is there that you will be interrogated by the Maquis.

When France surrendered to Germany on 22 June 1940, those who resented Germany occupation and the Vichy government formed cells that collectively were named the French Resistance. Called the Maquis in rural areas these groups were violent in nature, aiming to hurt or kill the German occupiers. Other teams used non-violent means, publishing underground newspapers, and broadcasted anti-German and anti-Vichy radio programs. Many of these cells were created after the 18 June 1940 address by Charles de Gaulle who encouraged the French people to continue the fight against the German forces even if the nation surrendered. To take advantage of these groups, the British Special Operations Executive (SOE) began infiltrating into France beginning in May 1941 to aid the resistance groups. (The southern part of France, except for the western half of Aquitaine along the Atlantic coast, became the zone libre ("free zone"), where the Vichy regime remained sovereign as an independent state, though under heavy German influence due to the restrictions of the Armistice and economic dependency on Germany).
Because de Gaulle always disagreed with his British allies, he formed his own agency to independently aid French resistance efforts without coordinating with British efforts. His efforts were a disaster, as the communists hated the General with a passion.

In the beginning, the resistance groups were scattered and lacked cooperation. On 22 June 1941, all communist groups in France merged into a larger group, showing the rest of the resistance groups the effectiveness of more coordinated resistance actions. On 11 November 1942, German forces marched to Vichy-held southern France, and the resistance sentiment spread into that region as well, especially after the Vichy government adopted some

German-influenced anti-Semitic policies. The initial German response was that of annoyance, and it soon turned into great frustration. "During the summer of 1941 the civilian population's resistance to our occupation forces intensified perceptibly in every theatre of war, with sabotage incidents and attacks on Germany security troops and installations", German Field Marshal Wilhelm Keitel recalled the reports that came to his desk during the war. "Sabotage became horrifying frequent in France and even in Belgium." To counter the resistance movement, German forces employed a policy to rule with an iron fist, including later savage retribution operations against innocent civilians.

The SS also tortured many suspected resistance group members, with them ending up either dead or in a concentration camp. Rarely, entire villages would be razed as deterrence to future acts of sabotage; such was the fate for Oradour-sur-Glane folk.

The Nazis brought a large box into the church and placed it in the centre of the women and children. They left, locked the door, and positioned themselves outside with guns aimed at all exits. The box soon exploded, filling the church with smoke. When the women and children tried to crawl through windows to escape the suffocating smoke and the scorching flames, they were shot by the waiting soldiers outside. While the makeshift bomb went off at the church, six groups of men were gunned down. The soldiers aimed their gunfire at the legs of their victims and then piled straw and wood on top of the fallen men. They then lit the straw on fire so that the wounded civilians were burnt alive. To disguise the massacre, the Nazis lit fires throughout the rest of the town. Only five men survived the massacre and only one woman from the church. Madame

Marguerite Rouffanche climbed out of a window and hid in a bush. She recovered from the gunshot wound she received during her escape. Adolf Hitler insisted that such draconian measures were necessary to deter the would-be "terrorists", otherwise the situation in France would become out of control.

Despite the risks, many resistance fighters continued to wield British supplied weapons to fight when the prospect of a cross-Channel invasion of France became closer to reality. The United States also began aiding the French Resistance. Their Office of Strategic Services (OSS) began sending its own, but badly trained unprofessional agents, into France supposedly to cooperate with the SOE to rally French support against German occupation. On 27 May 1943, after months of work, Jean Moulin persuaded several resistance groups to merge into the Conseil National de la Resistance (CNR), with Moulin becoming the first chairman of the alliance. On 21 June, however, Moulin was captured by the German Gestapo and was tortured to death. Henri Giraud and Charles de Gaulle became joint presidents of the CNR after the death of Moulin, but by October that year, the politically-minded de Gaulle was to maneuverer Giraud out of the position of power and became the sole leader of CNR. Although de Gaulle was difficult to work with for the Allied commanders, with him hiding in London, it was possible for the Allied command to pass orders for the resistance fighters to attack key communications and transportation targets to aid the planned Operation Overlord. Some 93 small teams of five agents (one American, three British, and one French) were then sent into France to closely coordinate actions immediately before the invasion. The resistance fighters continued to aid Allied invasion efforts after the forces had made footing on continental Europe.

Leaving his hotel so early in the morning attracted no attention. He had remembered to top up his fuel tank from a small fuel bowser parked amongst other military vehicles at the rear of Le Meurice, and the two officers raised the boom barrier without question to allow him to leave the confines of this deluxe military establishment. Apart from having to show his papers to over enthusiastic Feldgendarmerie, (military police) he was surprised at the ease of passing through control posts. Anton's kind bravado enabled lesser ranks to feel comfortable in his presence.

As arranged, he picked up Claire outside of the brothel, and off they sped in the direction of Versailles. He returned the occasional salute for idling solders returning from wherever who no doubt viewed his companion to be his French mistress.

The choices of which roads to take to Poitiers was open to discussion. By keeping to the anonymous country roads hopefully they would most possibly avoid any German interference but could be gunned down without question by a random Maquis cell. The main routes to Orleans, then Tours and onto Poitiers they would almost certainly encounter the movement of army traffic. Both agreed the latter route which was a smart move as there was little if any military convoys. Claire was told where to stop off-road outside of the town and wait for her contacts. Brutally two men jumped them both and each were summarily bound, gagged and blindfolded.

Four local Marquis paramilitaries manhandled the "Oberleutnant" into a room separate to where Claire was held. Still bound and blindfolded Anthony was aggressively interrogated and smacked around somewhat when they doubted his responses. His escape from the POW camp in Poland, his walk to Luxembourg, the dead German officer with pockets stuffed with Reichsmarks, and breakfast with William Joyce all seemed fanciful. However as soon as he spoke about his involvement as a printer in the production of Anti-Nazi posters and literature giving the name of the resistance operative, he dealt with together with his procurement of paper from the Catholic Church the atmosphere mellowed. Blindfold was removed and his hands were now freed to drink wine and break bread with his captors and with his lady Claire.

Wireless contact was established with the SOE in Paris, and facts given were corroborated with London and Luxembourg.

Two days later Anthony offered them his remaining German Marks, and surprisingly they asked if they could have his Oberleutnant uniform and his Volkswagen Type 82 Kübelwagen. "Tomorrow we will be heading to the crossing point into Spain. You will travel in the German uniform in the vehicle, and we will be your motorbike escort.

Only when we reach those who will get you out of France, we will you dress as a Basque (we have a beret for you and one for Claire), and then we will relieve you of your vehicle and your uniform. We need the car as we have something special planned in the New Year in Poitiers.

During December 1943 in World War II, there were several escape routes used by Allied airmen to cross from France to Spain. One of the most famous escape routes was known as the Comet Line (Le Réseau Comète). It was generally the Comet Line escorting Allied airmen down over the Pyrenees into Spain. The airmen were taken to the home of Katalina Aguirre at 58 Rue du Docteur Mice in Ciboure, a French seaside village in the German-occupied Basque Pyrenees.

The southern end of Hitler's "Atlantic Wall" was visible from Katalina's house, with German soldiers patrolling the shoreline. The escape plan involved crossing the Pyrenees with the help of Basque Mountain guide Florentino Goikoetxea.

Just as British airmen had done dozens of times before, Anthony and Claire hid in the loft of Katalina's house, preparing for their escape. From the loft window, they could see the ocean and the German coastal defences.

The plan was to escape over the Pyrenees with Florentino Goikoetxea, who would call as soon as it was dark. They rested during the day to conserve energy for the night's walk on 30 December 1943. Their Comet Line guide, Jean-Francois Nothomb (known as "Franco"), led them across the busy road bridge over the La Nivelle river to Ciboure. "Franco" befriended the German guard on the bridge, who remained unaware that Anthony and his girlfriend were crossing to Ciboure. (Below)

Once in Spain having dodged both the German frontier guards on the French side and the Spanish Police at the Basque border, they were escorted by the Spanish Comet Operatives and taken by pony and trap to the east of San Sebastian to meet up with a man and a clapped-out van from the Wolfram Mining Company. Anthony and Claire were on their way to meet up with her Uncle Damien in the Portuguese tungsten town of Panasqueira.

The journey would take 10 hours along some of the loneliest roads in Spain and Portugal. The 500-mile journey passed through Burgos a city in Spain located in the autonomous community of Castile and León. On to Palencia also located in the Northwest of the Iberian Peninsula. It being New Years Eve it was decided to overnight in Benavente. New Year's Eve 1943 revelry included a feast of lentil soup, unmarried ladies wearing red knickers, and just as the clock chimes, welcoming in 1944, for each bong everyone must eat a grape – twelve grapes in all – an almost impossible task. If a guy accepted a pair of red panties from a spinster, he had accepted her proposal of marriage. Claire wore no knickers as she was ready to pleasure her Anthony.

One New Years Day 1944 the roads were deserted so an early morning start heading southwest to Salamanca – famous for centuries of history, art and knowledge and the wonder of landmarks such as its famous university, one of the oldest in Europe. No time to discover the 1,000 mysteries of the town as they drive to Vilar Formoso the town and civil parish in the municipality of Almeida, Portugal. One of the most important crossings on the Portugal–Spain border. Just 75 miles to go to reach Uncle Damien in Panasqueira.

At the start of World War II in 1939, the Portuguese Government announced on 1 September that the 550-year-old Anglo-Portuguese Alliance remained intact, but since the British did not seek Portuguese assistance, Portugal was free to remain neutral in the war and would do so. In an aide-mémoire of 5 September 1939, the British government confirmed the understanding. As Adolf Hitler's occupation swept across Europe, neutral Portugal became one of Europe's last escape routes, and for Anthony this was now his opportunity to go home to England.

In August 1943, Portugal signed the Luso-British agreement, which leased bases in the Azores to the British. This was a key turning point in the Battle of the Atlantic, allowing the Allies to provide aerial coverage in the Mid-Atlantic gap; helping them to hunt U-boats and protect convoys. Churchill surprised members of parliament when he said he would use a 14th-century treaty; many MPs had not known that Portugal and England had the oldest operational alliance in the world, the Anglo-Portuguese Treaty of 1373. Churchill ended his speech saying: "I take this opportunity of placing on record the appreciation by His Majesty's Government, which I have no doubt is shared by Parliament and the British nation, of the attitude of the Portuguese Government, whose loyalty to their British Ally never wavered in the darkest hours of the war". Portugal also allowed the United Kingdom to buy Tungsten and receive credit backed by pounds sterling, assisting Great Britain to obtain vital goods at a time when it was short of gold and escudos and while all other neutrals were not prepared to trade sterling against gold. By 1945 the United Kingdom owed Portugal over £300 million under this arrangement.

Damien was so pleased to see his niece and thanked Anthony what seemed like a thousand times for including Claire in his escape plans. There was no time to spare, as the following evening the mv Margarethe freighter full to the gunnels with tungsten was due to depart Porto to cross the east of the Atlantic ocean passing through the Bay of Biscay into the Irish Sea along the western coast of the United Kingdom to the beautiful Bae Abergwaun the Welsh Pembrokeshire port of Fishguard. (During its life on the sea the ship was renamed the Olga, then Magda Maria and latterly Mi Amigo). Just a final night with Claire, his lovable agent provocateur, their adventures so special, their relationship initially commercial yet developing into fond appreciation. Claire would never travel to Britain, and Anthony would only visit Paris and Luxembourg briefly in future years. It was an explosively intimate time for both that embraced their souls for just a few weeks. To try to emulate the passions would be impossible and so were best left shelved somewhere in the canyons of their minds.

The voyage endured the roughest of rough seas and thirty-six hours on a freighter stinking of diesel oil could have been impossible except for the anaesthetic properties of three bottles of Kopke port, the world's oldest port house, gifted to Anthony by Damien for the crossing. This port has a bright amber colour with a brown-tawny halo. Elegant nose of dried fruits, well integrated with wood notes. Light and fragrant, with wonderful volume and structure. A wine with great freshness and multi-dimensional flavours. Delicate and persistent finish. Colheita, or single harvest Ports, are aged in the barrel. This is a contrast to vintage ports which are aged in the bottle and only have a short drinking window after opening. (If you could find a bottle today you would have to pay just shy of £2,000). At last Tony was back in Britain but who would believe the stories of his adventures, and whilst the war was still as brutal as ever, he would not, could not, or must not betray the confidences of those wonderful people who saved his life.

The Comet Line alone had successfully guided airmen, Jews and others of interest to the Nazis across the treacherous mountain range, providing a crucial escape route to neutral Spain. Anthony and Claire's dangerous journey to freedom involved courage, resourcefulness, and the assistance of brave individuals like Katalina and Florentino. The Comet Line remains one of the most inspiring stories of resistance during World War II, highlighting the resilience and determination of those who risked their lives to help others escape from occupied territories. It is understood that some 2,373 British and Commonwealth servicemen and 2,700 Americans reached Britain by escape lines, including Comet, during the Second World War. The Royal Air Forces Escaping Society estimated that 14,000 helpers worked with the many escape and evasion lines by 1944. (Réseau Comète; 1941–1944).

Shipping Tungsten (SS Margarethe)   **Radio Nord (SS Bon Jour)**

She was built as the schooner "Margarethe" for German owners. A sale in 1927 saw her lengthened in 1936. During the Second World War, she was requisitioned by the Kriegsmarine and served as an auxiliary ship between 1941 and 1943. In 1944 she was shipping Portuguese Tungsten to the U.K. By 1953, the ship was again lengthened, and then in 1959, converted to a floating Swedish radio station Radio Nord and renamed Bon Jour. Subsequently, she was registered as Magda Maria in 1961 and Mi Amigo in 1962. She served, intermittently, as a radio ship, until 1980, when she sank in a gale.

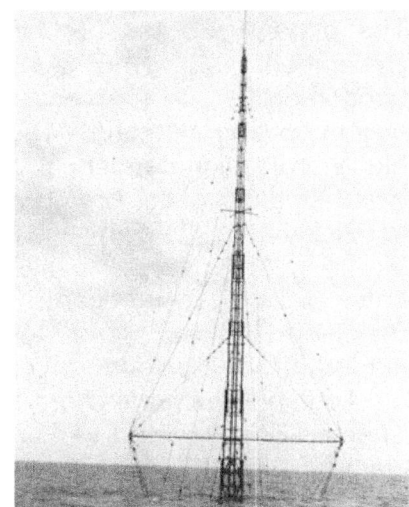

Radio Atlanta / Caroline South (Mi Amigo)   The Mi Amigo sinks 1980

Listening to historic recordings, the early programmes from Radio Caroline now sound bland, awkward and amateurish. But to the population, all day pop music radio was a revelation. No speeches, lectures, gardening tips or cookery suggestions. No 'Woman's Hour' or 'Listen With Mother.' No music shows where massed banjo bands murdered current pop hits. By the autumn of 1964 Caroline had more listeners than the three BBC networks combined.

The furious Alan Crawford put Radio Atlanta on air right next to Caroline's wavelength, but Caroline had the audience and a merger was inevitable. Crawford's ship stayed off Essex and became Caroline South, while the MV *Caroline* travelled to her original intended destination near the Isle Of Man and became Caroline North. Now O'Rahilly had almost all of the UK plus Southern Ireland and substantial parts of the continent in range of his transmitters.

With Caroline as the catalyst and its audience of tens of millions, new music and youth fashion accelerated at astonishing speed and hundreds of new bands achieved massive and sometimes lasting success. Jonathan King, broadcaster and pop pundit recalls his simple throwaway pop song 'Everyone's Gone To The Moon' that within weeks of initial air play on Caroline projected him from obscurity to starring on prime time television at the prestigious London Palladium. Unknown actor Simon Dee, head hunted from Caroline, became one of the first superstar chat show hosts on British TV.

The blatant success of Caroline made imitation inevitable. In December 1964 the American backed and styled Radio London arrived on the vessel *Galaxy*. While Caroline could later claim perseverance and longevity, Radio London (Big L) delivered highly professional American programming that temporarily at least captured much of the audience of Caroline South requiring Caroline to quickly adapt its own style and format.

Later two more American influenced stations Britain Radio and Swinging Radio England went on air from one ship. Radio 270 started off the Yorkshire coast while Radio Scotland on board the old lightship *Comet* anchored off the Scottish East coast. In the Thames Estuary were various marine structures which had been wartime sea forts. Abandoned by the military they made excellent and stable transmitting platforms and were quickly boarded and claimed by further radio entrepreneurs. Soon Radio 390 an easy listening station and the most powerful of all the sixties offshore broadcasters was on air, while from other structures Radio Essex and Radio King started transmissions.

From the day that Caroline appeared the UK government made threatening noises but no serious action was taken. Now there were several independent broadcasters sending programmes into the UK and twenty million people were listening. Further stations were rumoured to be in preparation and for the government things were getting out of hand. It was a delicate matter trying to legislate against a pastime which was providing a third of the population with the best fun they had enjoyed in a long time.

It is a remarkable coincidence that the freighter that took Tony Atkinson back to the UK from Portugal was subsequently lengthened and adapted to broadcast popular music to a variety of European countries. Such a mirrored image that Radio Luxembourg operated before, during and after WWII.

The original Caroline ship, the mv Frederica, at anchor off of the Isle of Man with the call sign Radio Caroline North

Radio Nord serving Scandinavia, then refitted for Radio Atlanta and becoming Radio Caroline South anchored off the Essex Coast

CHAPTER THIRTEEN

FOR YOU ANTHONY, A JOB AT THE B.B.C.

The BBC's Monitoring Service was created in 1939 on the outset of WWII, its purpose was, and still is today, to gather and interpret international news as rapidly and economically as possible. Although BBC reporters were embedded with British troops in various theatres of war their job was to report on the progress of our military, and not to listen to foreign propaganda. Richard Dimbleby (below) was one of the Corporation's finest radio journalists reporting throughout WWII from the front line up to the horrors of Belsen concentration camp.

Initially employing several hundred 'monitors', many of them refugees, the service rapidly expanded so that it could 'listen' 24 hours a day to all the European languages likely to be of wartime use. The BBC and wider world quickly recognised the uniqueness and value of BBC Monitoring, calling it in 1940 'a modern Tower of Babel'. Churchill was an avid customer of the service, and would ring up in the middle of the night and ask (of Hitler) 'What's that fellow been saying?'

The organisation played an important role in helping observers keep track of developments post WWII, including the Cold War, the disintegration of the Iron Curtain and collapse of the Soviet Union. Also monitored were the Falklands conflict, Yugoslav wars, and Middle East hostilities. Over the years, BBC Monitoring has innovated and developed, now monitoring over 3,000 sources (across radio, TV, press, internet, and news agencies), in 100 languages and across 150 countries. Its purpose remains to observe, understand, and explain to the world's media, and so help Britain and her international audiences follow and interpret key events.

Initially based in London then Evesham, BBC Monitoring moved in 1943 to Caversham Park near Reading, where it was based until moving to Broadcasting House London in 2018. It was to Caversham Park that Anthony was seconded. When he disembarked at Fishguard, still being a Sherwood Forrester soldier, he made his way to the regimental headquarters in Derby. Having explained what happened after he escaped from the Polish POW camp, their senior officer realising that he was multilingual and had experienced more than any other army private Anthony was invited to visit the BBC Monitoring people in Caversham. Made up to the rank of Sergeant it was there that he would spend the next ten years up to and including VE day in 1945 and throughout the major tension period of the Cold War up to 1953.

When British Prime Minister Winston Churchill, Soviet Premier Joseph Stalin, and US President Harry Truman got together in July 1945 in the German town of Potsdam to discuss the fate of Germany, the meeting underlined the differences between the Allied powers and set the stage for a post-war "cold" war that would be waged for more than fifty years between two global superpowers.

Meanwhile in France the resistance organisations were receiving huge deliveries of arms and ammunition from the British as rumours were circulating around on the possibility of an Allied invasion. Established by ordinance on 17 September 1943 by the CFLN, it held its first meetings in Algiers, at the Palais Carnot (the former headquarters of the Financial Delegations), between 3 November 1943 and 25 July 1944. On 3 June 1944 it was placed under the authority of the Provisional Government of the French Republic (GPRF), which succeeded the French Committee of National Liberation (CFLN). In his inaugural speech, de Gaulle, who had flown in from London on 3 November 1943 gave the body his imprimatur, as providing a means of representing the people of France as democratically and legally as possible under difficult and unparalleled circumstances, until such time as democracy could once again be restored. As an indication of the importance he attached to the body, de Gaulle participated in about twenty sessions of the Consultative Assembly in Algiers.

In January 1944, General Dwight Eisenhower was appointed commander of Operation Overlord. In the months and weeks before D-Day, the Allies carried out a massive deception operation intended to make the Germans think the main invasion target was

Pas-de-Calais (the narrowest point between Britain and France) rather than Normandy. In addition, they led the Germans to believe that Norway and other locations were also potential invasion targets. Many tactics were used to carry out the deception, including fake equipment; a phantom army commanded by George Patton and supposedly based in England, across from Pas-de-Calais; double agents; and fraudulent radio transmissions. On 1 February the Supreme Command met in London.

Front Row: Air Chief Marshal Sir Arthur W Tedder, Deputy Supreme Commander, Expeditionary Force; General Dwight Eisenhower, Supreme Commander, Expeditionary Force; General Sir Bernard Montgomery, Commander in Chief, 21st Army Group. Back Row: Lieutenant General Omar Bradley, Commander in Chief, US 1st Army; Admiral Sir Bertram H Ramsay, Allied Naval Commander in Chief, Expeditionary Force; Air Chief Marshal Sir Trafford Leigh-Mallory, Allied Air Commander in Chief, Expeditionary Force; and far right Lieutenant General Walter Bedell-Smith, Chief of Staff to Eisenhower.

The German Army high command had long been expecting an Allied invasion of northern France but had no means of knowing where precisely the stroke would come: while Rundstedt, commander in chief in the west, thought that the landings would be made between Calais and Dieppe (at the narrowest width of the

Channel between England and France), Hitler prophetically indicated the central and more westerly stretches of the coast of Normandy as the site of the attack; and Rommel, who was in charge of the forces on France's Channel coast, finally came around to Hitler's opinion. The fortifications of those stretches were consequently improved, but Rundstedt and Rommel still took different views about the way in which the invasion should be met: while Rundstedt recommended a massive counterattack on the invaders after their landing, Rommel, fearing that Allied air supremacy might interfere fatally with the adequate massing of the German forces for such a counterattack, advocated instead immediate action on the beaches against any attempted landing. The Germans had 59 divisions spread over western Europe from the Low Countries to the Atlantic and Mediterranean coasts of France; but approximately half of this number was static, and the remainder included only 10 armoured or motorized divisions. Postponed from May, the western Allies' "Operation Overlord," their long-debated invasion of northern France, took place on 6 June 1944.

Eisenhower selected 5 June 1944, as the date for the invasion; however, bad weather on the days leading up to the operation caused it to be delayed for 24 hours. Group Captain James Stagg of the Royal Air Force met Eisenhower on the evening of 4 June. He and his meteorological team predicted that the weather would improve enough for the invasion to proceed on 6 June. The next available dates with the required tidal conditions (but without the desirable full moon) would be two weeks later, from 18 to 20 June. Postponement of the invasion would have required recalling men and ships already in position to cross the English Channel and would have increased the chance that the invasion plans would be detected. Eisenhower gave the go-ahead for Operation Overlord as advised by the RAF for 6 June. He told the troops: "You are about to embark upon the Great Crusade, toward which we have striven these many months. The eyes of the world are upon you."

Later that day, more than 5,000 ships and landing craft carrying troops and supplies left England for the trip across the Channel to France, while more than 11,000 aircraft were mobilized to provide air cover and support for the invasion.

By dawn on 6 June thousands of paratroopers and glider troops were already on the ground behind enemy lines, securing bridges and exit roads. The amphibious invasions began at 6:30am. The British and Canadians overcame light opposition to capture beaches codenamed Gold, Juno, and Sword, as did the Americans at Utah Beach. U.S. forces faced the heaviest of resistance at Omaha Beach, where there were over 2,000 American casualties. However, by the day's end, approximately 156,000 Allied troops had successfully stormed Normandy's beaches. According to some estimates, more than 4,000 Allied troops lost their lives in the D-Day invasion, with thousands more wounded or missing.

In less than a week later, on 11 June, the beaches were fully secured and over 326,000 troops, plus more than 50,000 vehicles and some 100,000 tons of equipment had landed at Normandy.

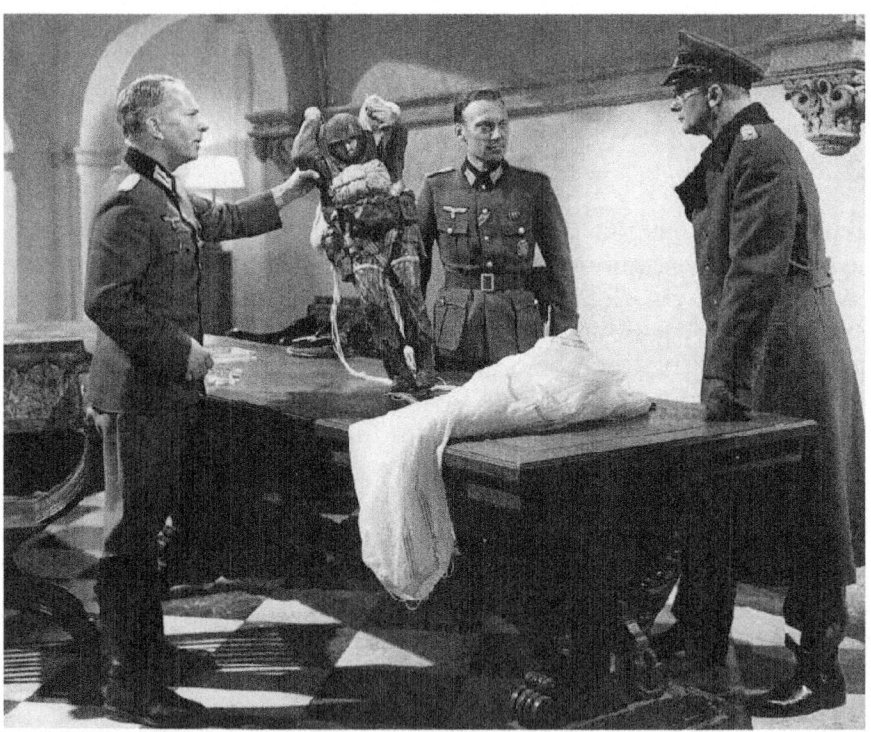

D-Day dummies were dropped by the RAF dressed in paratrooper uniforms, including boots and helmets. In addition to the parachutes strapped to their burlap backs, each Rupert carried recordings of gunfire and exploding mortar rounds adding to the authenticity of the simulated air attack. Drawstrings at the top of the head, wrists, and ankles allowed the dummy to be filled with straw or sand. Operation Titanic kicked off late at night on 5 June 1944. There were three drop zones, all located north of the Seine. Two hundred dummies were dropped into the Yerville-Doudeville-FauvilleYvetot area, 50 dummies landed around Maltot, and another 200 were dumped near Marigny. A few hundred other "dolls" what today we would brand as "Action Men" were tossed out randomly to add to the confusion.To ensure things went as planned, a team of human paratroopers from the British Special Air Service plummeted to the ground alongside their cloth counterparts. The real soldiers added additional special effects, including flares, chemicals to simulate the smell of exploded shells, and amplified battle sounds. When the Ruperts landed, they would self-destruct, exploding into pieces and leaving just a charred white parachute behind.

Operation Fortitude was another elaborate, mind-boggling hoax – using decoys such as rubber tanks, canvas ships, plywood aircraft, and even dummy soldiers to fool the Germans about where we secretly planned to land on D-Day.

Everyone knew the Allies would eventually try to take back the continent. But for the German Military the question was when, and where? Pas-de-Calais was just thirty miles away from England's coastline, so it made perfect sense that the Allies would invade Calais. But in fact, they secretly selected the beaches of Normandy, about one hundred miles away. The early hours of 6 June 1944 was the date for the second hoax But to keep the destination under wraps, an elaborate plan called Operation Fortitude used multiple layers of trickery. It cannot be disputed that this so dastardly clever and

striking - the creation of two phantom armies – one in Scotland to threaten an invasion of Norway, and the other in southeast England to assume a Pas-de-Calais attack. The idea for a fake army was a stroke of genius, because the Germans believed he would play a major role in the invasion. A team of "camofleurs" and British film set designers was brought on board to mock up an entire fake army on the coast around Dover, the closest point to Calais. They created what was basically a rubber and straw army of tanks, anti-aircraft gun emplacements, ships and "Action Men".

For their part, the Germans suffered from confusion in the ranks and the absence of celebrated commander Rommel, who was away on leave. At first, Hitler, believing the invasion was a hoax designed to distract the Germans from a coming attack north of the Seine River, refused to release nearby divisions to join the counterattack. Reinforcements had to be called from further afield, causing delays. He also hesitated in calling for armoured divisions to help in the defence. Moreover, the Germans were hampered by aggressive Allied air support, which took out many key bridges and forced the Germans to reroute and take long detours, as well as efficient Allied naval support, which helped protect advancing Allied troops.

In the ensuing weeks, the Allies fought their way across the Normandy countryside in the face of determined German resistance, as well as a dense landscape of marshes and hedgerows. By the end of June, the Allies had seized the vital port of Cherbourg, landed approximately 850,000 men and 150,000 vehicles in Normandy, and were poised to continue their march across France.

By the end of August 1944, the Allies had reached the Seine River, Paris was liberated, and the Germans had been removed from northwestern France, effectively concluding the Battle of Normandy. The Allied forces then prepared to enter Germany, where they would meet up with Soviet troops moving in from the east.

The Normandy invasion began to turn the tide against the Nazis. A significant psychological blow, it also prevented Hitler from sending troops from France to build up his Eastern Front against the advancing Soviets.

All this activity was followed and documented by Anthony and the BBC Monitoring services in Caversham Park.

After reducing the Falaise Pocket in Normandy, on 19 August 1944 the Allied armies advanced swiftly to Rouen and Nantes, where a bridgehead was established on the Seine. In the meantime, on 18 August Paris had taken up arms. General de Gaulle had planned for General Leclerc's 2nd Armoured Division to liberate the capital.

According to the Allied plans, Paris was not a military objective, and the city should be bypassed. But General de Gaulle, the head of the Provisional Government of the French Republic, saw the liberation of the capital as symbolic and hence considered it a political objective: Paris must be liberated by French soldiers. De Gaulle wanted to be seen as the leader of a country that liberated itself by its own efforts. Moreover, with the bombing of strategic junctions in northern the German forces' withdrawal to the east, and to the Americans as they continued to advance north and eastwards.

Across the city, the Resistance built barricades. The police turned the Paris police headquarters into a stronghold. There were violent clashes between the Germans and the Resistance, integrated in the FFI. On 20 August, a ceasefire was called, thanks to the Swedish consul, Raoul Nordling. But the very next day, on a decision of the Parisian liberation committee, the truce was broken, and the street fighting resumed. The poorly armed Resistance fighters faced 20,000 German troops equipped with tanks and supported by aircraft, under the command of General von Choltitz, appointed head of "Groß-Paris". For Hitler, "Paris must not fall into the hands of the enemy except as a field of ruins." On 21 August, an envoy sent by Rol-Tanguy managed to cross the German lines and warn Leclerc: Allied intervention was needed, or else the Parisian revolt would end in a bloodbath. While General von Choltitz's men tried to regain control of the city, on 22 August General Eisenhower agreed that the French 2nd DB, together with the US 4th Infantry Division, should make a rush for Paris. In late afternoon, a Piper light aircraft, piloted by Captain Callet of the 2nd DB, flew over the city and his observer, Lieutenant Mantoux, threw a "Stand Firm We Are On The Way" message from Leclerc into the police headquarters' courtyard.

On the morning of 23 August, the 2nd DB France's 2nd Armoured Division (French: 2e Division Blindée, 2e DB) supported on its right flank by the US 4th Division, set out. The Germans had formed a solid line of defence from Trappes to Fresnes, south of Paris. Violent fighting took place in Palaiseau, Champlan, Toussus-le-Noble, Jouy-en-Josas, Clamart, Longjumeau, Wissous, Fresnes and Antony. On 24 August, the entire division was stalled by German "hedgehogs" (anti-tank obstacles,) outside Paris. At the junction of Croix-de-Berny, congested with the division's vehicles, Leclerc hastened the advance of his units and, at 7.30pm, decided to send a detachment to Paris under the command of Captain Dronne, with three tanks, half-tracks and 150 men.

At nightfall on 24 August 1944, the first soldiers of the 2nd DB entered Paris, by the Porte d'Italie. They were the 9th Company of the Chad Infantry Regiment, or the "Nueve", comprising 146 Spanish Republicans or Hispanic men of a total of 160. Followed up by three Sherman tanks of the 501st Combat Tank Regiment, Dronne reached city hall at 8.45 pm. There he met Bidault, Luizet and Chaban-Delmas. French radio announced the 2nd DB's arrival. The great bell of Notre-Dame rang out.

At dawn on 25 August, the 2nd DB entered Paris by the Porte de Saint-Cloud, Porte d'Orléans, Porte de Gentilly and Porte d'Italie. Leclerc went through the Porte d'Orléans, met Chaban-Delmas at Place Denfert-Rochereau, then made his way down the Avenue du Maine to Gare Montparnasse station, where he set up his command post. Meanwhile, the 4th US Infantry Division entered Paris by the Porte d'Iyalie.

The people of Paris were surprised to see French soldiers and gave them an enthusiastic welcome. The harried Germans took refuge in a small number of strongpoints. But the fighting was difficult and bloody at Place de la Concorde, Place de l'Étoile, Place de la République, at the Bastille and on Boulevard Saint-Germain.

The largest strongpoint on the Left Bank of the Seine was the Palais du Luxembourg covered with small blockhouses and guarded by tanks where fierce fighting pitched Germans against the Resistance fighters.

Hôtel Meurice, where Anthony stayed as **Oberleutnant Anton Heidelberg,** was attacked, and von Choltitz and his senior commanders were captured.

At around 4pm, in the staff apartment of police chief Luizet, the German general signed the act of surrender. Then he was taken to Gare Montparnasse, where he signed the order for ceasefire, which was circulated to the 20 German strongpoints still fighting.

Colonel Rol-Tanguy co-signed the act of capitulation and western France, Paris was one of the few communication hubs to remain intact, again monitored by Anthony at the BBC.

General von Choltitz signs the surrender document at the Préfecture de Police on 25 August. (Photographie de Société nationale des chemins de fer Français courtesy of SNCF - Paris Musées)

Shortly afterwards, Leclerc explained the situation to General de Gaulle, who had just arrived from isolation away from the war zone. While members of the National Council of the Resistance (CNR) and the Parisian Committee for Liberation (CPL) awaited him at city hall, de Gaulle headed for the war ministry, at Rue Saint-Dominique, to assume control and make known the re-establishment of State authority. It was not until 7pm that he made his way to city hall, where he made what has since become a famous speech. Paris was liberated at a cost of a thousand FFI casualties, 582 civilians killed and over 2,000 wounded, and 156 soldiers of the 2nd DB killed and 225 injured. The enemy sustained 3,200 dead, while 12,800 were taken prisoner.

On 26 August, General de Gaulle visited the Arc de Triomphe, where he laid a wreath on the Tomb of the Winston Churchill with members of the government,

CNR and senior French military leaders and Winston Churchill.

Elated crowds of Parisians gathered all along the route taken by de Gaulle to Notre-Dame cathedral, cheering him and legitimating him as leader. The presence of English-language press and radio reporters meant considerable coverage of the event around the world. Euphoric scenes took place in London, New York, Montreal, Chicago and in the streets of Montevideo and Buenos Aires. The liberation of the "City of Light" symbolised the imminent defeat of Germany and Nazism.

Then retribution of those assumed to have cooperated with the Germans. Nazi collaborators were the first to be prosecuted and punished for their crimes against the French nation. A wave of pursuits of traitors occurred, followed by executions of those tied to the Nazi regime. The first which included convictions, public executions, and humiliation of the suspected traitors. The second, known as the legal purge, began when Charles de Gaulle, head of the Provisional Government of the French Republic, started a campaign of legal pursuits of the collaborators. As in many other occupied countries, France had domestic traitors who collaborated with the Nazi regime.

This partnership with the enemy was driven by various factors, such as racism, opportunism, and hatred for communism, but there were also people forced to work with the Germans. The main collaborator was the Vichy government, which controlled the occupied part of France as a puppet government for the Nazis. Marshal Philippe Pétain and Pierre Laval were the heads of the regime, responsible for the deportation of 76,000 Jews to the extermination camps built by their government. Gypsies, political opponents, and homosexuals were also sent to the death camps. Official reports state that only 2,500 of the Jews that were deported survived the war. These Nazi collaborators committed some of the worst crimes of the war and approximately 120,000 people sentenced to various punishments.

Pétain dispatched an emissary to arrange for a peaceful transfer of power. De Gaulle refused to receive the envoy. Brought to trial in France (below) for his behaviour after 1940, he was condemned to death in August 1945. His sentence was immediately commuted to solitary confinement for life. He was imprisoned in a fortress on the Île d'Yeu off the Atlantic coast, where he died at the age of 95.

Bystanders began to gather early on the Monday morning of 23 July 1945 outside the gates protecting the courtyard of the Palais de Justice in Paris for the trial of **Marshal Philippe Pétain**. There were not many, as it was known that few places would be available for the public. The building was protected by 600 police officers, one of whom tried to satisfy disappointed punters by dangling the consolation prize of the trial of the "Georgian Gestapo", a band of foreigners who had perpetrated gruesome acts of atrocity during the occupation. Seats were available. That morning, police were even stationed on the roof of the Sainte-Chapelle. The previous night seven prisoners – collaborators awaiting trial, according to some reports, common criminals according to others – had escaped from their cells in the dépôt, climbed through a central-heating pipe, clambered on to the roof of the Palais and jumped down to the quay below. No one believed that the Marshal, however sprightly, would be capable of a similar feat, but this incident had been an embarrassment.

French novelist Louis-Ferdinand Céline, who supported the Axis forces and wrote anti-Semitic pamphlets during the war was also imprisoned. People who profited during the war were assassinated. An estimated 6,000 executions were carried out before France was liberated, and another 4,000 occurred after the country was freed. The pursuits were carried out by both individuals and organizations. Nazi-hunting groups were established, tasked with gathering information and tracking down the suspected Nazi supporters.

Civilians helped the authorities by providing information about suspects they had seen and recognised.

Many women who were suspected of having romantic relations with German soldiers or were prostitutes that provided their services to the enemy, were disgracefully punished, and humiliated by having their heads shaved publicly. These girls, the majority of which had risked their lives by passing information to the resistance and the British SOE spies embedded all over France. Their "pillow talk" together with the ladies having the opportunity to go through the pockets of their "spent" clients as they were sleeping, was the most invaluable of source for future Nazi planning. Anthony was thrilled that he was able to get Claire out of Paris before this madness kicked off.

After Paris, city after city in France was freed of Nazi occupation. As the liberation progressed, resistance groups supported by the troops of French Army B, from the Département de Algeria were incorporated into the Allied strength. In September, under threat of the Allied advance, Pétain and the remains of the Vichy regime fled into exile in Germany. The Allied armies continued to push the Germans back through eastern France and in February 1945, back across the Rhine into Germany.

CHAPTER FOURTEEN

BATTLING THE BULGE AND AFTER

Firstly, the timeline continued with an event called "the greatest American battle of the war" by Winston Churchill. The Battle of the Bulge in the Ardennes region of Belgium was Adolf Hitler's last major offensive in World War II against the Western Front. Hitler's aim was to split the Allies in their drive toward Germany. The German troops' failure to divide Britain, France and America with the Ardennes offensive paved the way to victory for the allies. Lasting six brutal weeks, from the 16 December 1944 to 25 January 1945, the assault, also called the Battle of the Ardennes, took place during frigid weather conditions, with some 30 German divisions attacking battle-fatigued American troops across 85 miles of the densely wooded Ardennes Forest.

As the Germans drove into the Ardennes, the Allied line took on the appearance of a large bulge, giving rise to the battle's name. The battle proved to be the costliest ever fought by the U.S. Army, which suffered over 100,000 casualties. The formerly serene, wooded region of Ardennes was hacked into chaos by fighting as the Americans dug in against the German advance at St.-Vith, Elsenborn Ridge, Houffalize and, later, Bastogne, which was defended by the 101st Airborne Division. American troops advance on a German machine gun position in the Ardennes.

Hitler's aim was to split the Allies in their drive toward Germany. The German troops' failure to divide Britain, France and America with the Ardennes offensive paved the way to victory for the allies. German troops pass burning US equipment. Freezing rain, thick fog, deep snow drifts and record-breaking low temperatures brutalized the American troops. Here, soldiers of the 2nd Infantry Division lie flat in the snow to avoid enemy mortar fire in Ondenval, Belgium 16 January 1945.

American GI's helped fleeing residents load their belongings and themselves on trucksin a lull in the last days of the Battle of the Bulge.

The surprise German attack broke through the front on day one as stories quickly spread of massacred soldiers and civilians, according to the U.S. Army Centre of Military History. For those who had lived through 1940, the picture was all too familiar. Belgian townspeople put away their Allied flags and brought out their swastikas. Police in Paris enforced an all-night curfew. British veterans waited nervously to see how the Americans would react to a full-scale German offensive, and British generals quietly acted to safeguard the Meuse River's crossings. Even American civilians, who had thought final victory was near were sobered by the Nazi onslaught. Hitler's mid-December timing of the attack, one of the bloodiest of the war, was strategic, as freezing rain, thick fog, deep snow drifts and record-breaking low temperatures brutalized the American troops. More than 15,000 "cold injuries" including trench foot, pneumonia, and frostbite were reported that winter.

The US Army troops got word that the Germans had dropped a lot of paratroopers behind our lines, and that they were dressed like American soldiers and spoke English. They were there to create confusion and the Germans also changed road signs and spread misinformation. The Nazis were carefully groomed for their dangerous mission. They spoke excellent English, and their slang had been tuned up by close association with American prisoners of war in German camps. Under the rules of the Hague Convention these Germans were classifiable as spies and subject to an immediate court martial by a military tribunal. After brief deliberation American officers found them guilty and ordered the usual penalty for spies: death by firing squad. To stop infiltrators, the U.S. troops would ask suspected Germans to answer American trivia questions.

"Three times I was ordered to prove my identity," General Omar

Bradley (left) recalled, "The first time by identifying Springfield as the capital of Illinois; the second by locating the guard between the centre and the tackle on a line of scrimmage; the third by naming the then-current spouse of a blonde named Betty Grable." It wasn't until Christmas Day that the weather conditions finally cleared, allowing Allied air forces to strike. It was on that bright, clear and cold Christmas morning in 1944 that the ground froze solid. The tanks and air forces could finally manoeuvre and get assistance to all of us who were previously blocked off. It was a welcome sign to see the sun come up, and everyone joked that they were alive for one more day.

General Dwight D. Eisenhower, the supreme Allied commander, and General George S. Patton led the American defence to restore the front. Eisenhower gave Patton the Third Army, about 230,000 soldiers, and ordered him to head to the Ardennes.

In the small, pivotal Belgian town of Bastogne, the Germans surrounded thousands of Allied troops. Eisenhower, in response, sent in more units, including the famed 101st Airborne Division. When the Germans sent a message demanding the surrender of the 101st on 22 December they got a one-word response from its commander, Brig. Gen. Anthony McAuliffe: 'Nuts!' This was interpreted by German officers as a more colourful and negative response to their demand. The day after Christmas, units of Patton's rapidly approaching Third Army finally arrived, broke through the German lines, and rescued the troops. Claiming victory of the battle on 25 January 1945, the Allies headed for Berlin. The war ended less than five months later with Germany's 7 May 1945 surrender following Hitler's suicide to escape from the ravages of the advancing Russian army that has surrounded his bunker.

In all, according to the **U.S. Department of Defence,** more than a million soldiers took part in this battle. That included 600,000 Germans, 500,000 Americans, and 54,000 British, one battalion of Canadians under British command all fought in the Battle of the Bulge, with approximately 19,000 soldiers killed in action, 47,500 wounded and 23,000-plus missing. About 100,000 Germans were killed, wounded, or captured.

The Ardennes campaign of 1944-45 was only one in a series of difficult engagements in the battle for Europe, Nevertheless, it can be said that the Ardennes campaign epitomised them all. For it was here American and British soldiers suffered their most casualties.

Pictures courtesy of the National archives New Orleans

BATTLE OF THE BULGE : AS IT HAPPENED

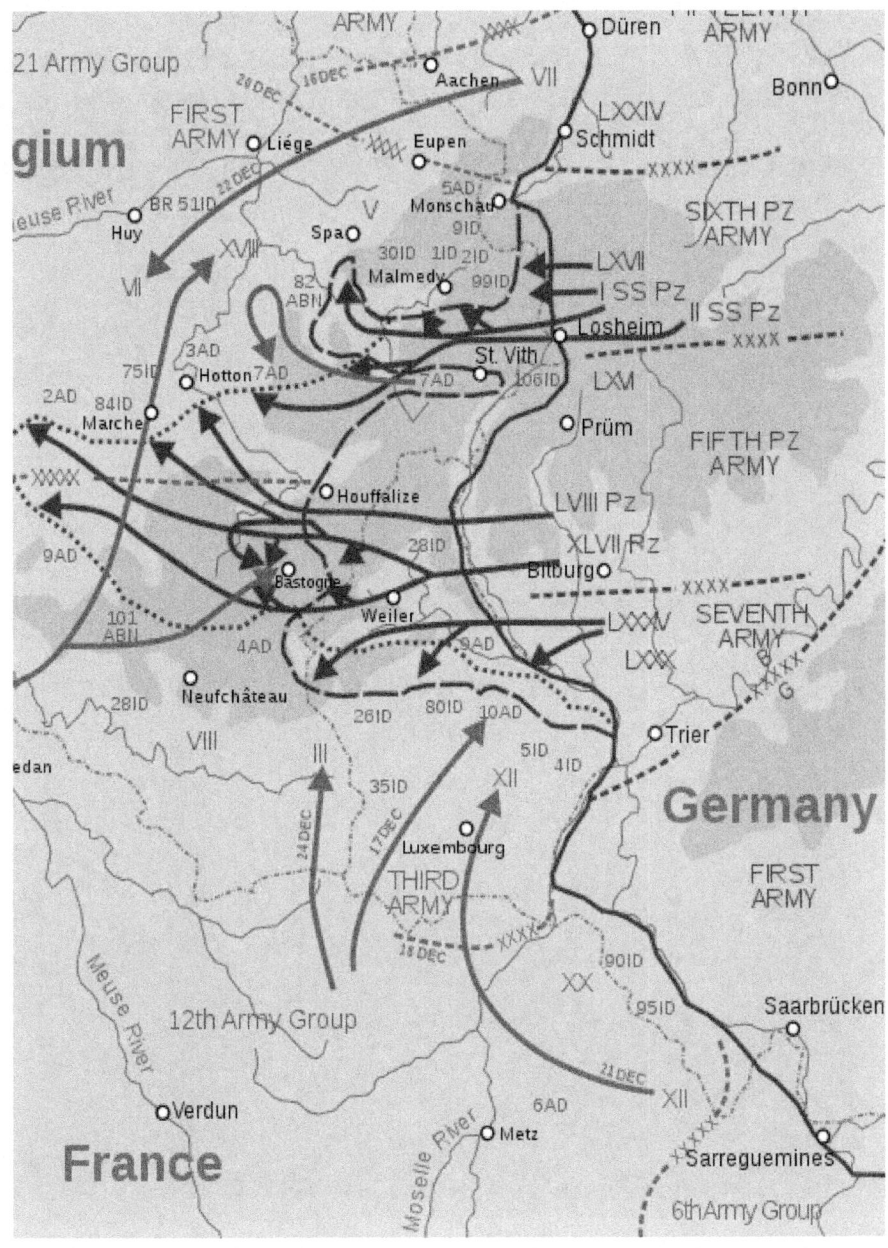

AUTHOR'S PERSONAL JOURNEY

Many former members of the Queen Mary's Army Auxiliary Corps (QMAAC) joined the Auxiliary Territorial Service (ATS), which was formed in September 1938, including the author's birth mother.

Somewhere in Belgium

Somewhere in Belgium, we landed one day
We saw Ostend and Aalst, and then
right here we had to stay.
It isn't a village, it isn't a town
It's just a gunsite where we
settled down.

It's just a gunsite with gunners
and guns.
And number 10 and 584 all help to fool
the huns.
But we never grumble, just say it's a
pest
When doodle bugs pass us, and "jim"
gives us rest.

And we curse when our Sgts say
"water".
For we know what that means from
the start.
Then we fill all the cans in our
quarters
and then we empty the water cart

Somewhere in Belgium, we're thinking of
you.
And there by candle light, we try to write
a line or two.
And then when as we're manning
Our thoughts ever stray.
Over the water, down old Blighty
Way.

(Above: Letter from Betty Doreen Gitsham 1944 somewhere in
Belgium) My son Geoff filled in a form to increase the parameters
of his life insurance cover following the birth of Sophie my
granddaughter . He declared that his dad, that's me, had had a

heart transplant in 1994 at the Papworth Hospital. In a heartbeat, literally, he was no longer insured. Geoff's insurers said that he would remain uninsurable until they had sight of my parents' medical records. Ada and John were my mum and dad and I had no interest in spending money with the Mormons who "own" Ancestry.com the privately held online company based in Lehi, Utah with links to the Church of the Latter Day Saints.

The largest for-profit genealogy company in the world, operates a network of genealogical, historical records, and related genetic genealogy websites. (As of November 2018, the company claimed to provide access to approximately 10 billion historical records, to have 3 million paying subscribers, and to have sold 14 million DNA kits to customer. In 2019, Ancestry.com received the German Big Brother Award, a negative recognition "for exploiting an interest in genealogy to entice people into submitting saliva samples" in other words to pile up a treasure trove of genome data for commercial research, because that is their actual business model.)

I had understood that my birth mother was a 15-year-old Irish girl, my biological father was a GI and rubbing my hands with glee I thought that this would enable me to get my hands upon an Irish Passport, if not a "green card".

To start the process was easy. A couple of emails to my local authority, a meeting with a councillor and I am informed that my birth mother was Betty Doreen Gitsham of Totnes in Devon. I was born in a "waifs and strays" home in Southport, so I am not Irish - I am a "scouser".

The heart-wrenching part of this procedure was not finding the details of my biological parentage but reading the court applications for my adoption by my mum and dad. "A non-parlour type of house, clean and comfortable. Male applicant is a bricklayer on £6 a week, rent and rates 15/1d – owner tenants. Infant has been in custody of applicants for 6 months."

Betty had moved from Southport to Loughborough to be close to a friend, and my mum and dad went on the bus from Leicester to Loughborough to collect me. That must have been a mixture of emotions for all concerned.

My given name at the time of birth was Brian William Gitsham. Betty married William Clarke. (My adopted name at the time of my christening became Brian John Slaughter, John being my dad's name. Mind you Dad had two names, John George Slaughter and Jack Weeks which is still a mystery.)

I have learnt that Betty my birth mother was in the women's army during the second world war. Private Gitsham W/112204 was based not far from Ostend as was listed as being an anti-aircraft gunner. True to rumour my biological father was a GI in the US Army, so I was conceived in Belgium on or around 13 March 1945, yet he is not named on my birth certificate, possibly because it was protocol for the US military not to admit to having sired children whilst in conflict. I am classed by the American government as "spoils of war", or more commonly referred to in the UK as a "bastard." It was in this area that my birth father would have returned after taking part in the "Battle of the Bulge, " impregnating young Betty before heading back into Bastogne and then into Luxembourg with his battalion in a clean-up operation – 85% were known not to have survived.

In March 1945, during the final stages of WWII in Europe, significant events unfolded in Belgium. Terlanenveld, a nondescript field near Brussels, served as one of the largest prisoner-of-war (POW) camps in western Europe. From March 1945 to August 1946, it held nearly 60,000 German prisoners of war. This camp was part of more than 40 POW and labour camps established by the Allies in Belgium after Germany's surrender. American troops played a crucial role in the liberation of Belgium. Despite mixed reception, they came to symbolize a "modern" liberation, creating rising expectations among the Belgian population.

On 2 and 3 March 1945, No. 427 Squadron conducted its last sorties on Halifax IIIs. About a week later, on 11 March 1, the squadron's Lancaster Is and IIIs received their operational baptism against the enemy. These historical events reflect the complex dynamics of wartime Europe and the pivotal role played by various forces during that critical period. The Belgian population's reaction to the arrival of American troops during World War II was a mix of emotions and expectations. For many Belgians, the sight of American soldiers symbolised liberation from German occupation. The arrival of Allied forces, including the Americans, brought hope for a better future after years of hardship and oppression. Belgians of course expressed gratitude toward the American troops who risked their lives to free their country. Celebrations erupted in the streets as people welcomed the liberators with cheers, waving flags, and offering food and drinks. However, not everyone greeted the Americans with open arms as some Belgians were wary of the sudden change and the uncertainties that came with it. There were concerns about how the post-war period would unfold and whether the promises of freedom and prosperity would be fulfilled. The arrival of American troops created rising expectations among the Belgian population and people hoped for a swift return to normality, economic recovery, and democratic governance. The Belgian population's reaction to American troops was a blend of relief, gratitude, cautious optimism, and high hopes for a brighter future. Now it was Holland's turn for the Allies to rid the Dutch of five years of Nazi occupation.

The Netherlands were liberated by Canadian forces, three British infantry divisions, the 1st Polish Armoured Division, American, Belgian, Dutch and Czechoslovak troops and parts of the country. In particular the south-east, was liberated by the British Second Army which included American, Polish airborne forces and French Airborne's crews. In late March, as other Allied armies crossed the Rhine into Germany, the First Canadian Army began rooting out German forces in the remainder of the Netherlands. The Canadians faced stiff fighting in places, and were also hampered by the broken roads, bridges and other infrastructure destroyed by the fleeing Germans, who blew up some of the dykes in the western Netherlands, flooding parts of the countryside. The Canadians and the Brits were greeted as heroes as they liberated small towns and major cities, including Amsterdam, Rotterdam and The Hague. Millions of Dutch had suffered terribly during the harsh "hunger winter" of 1945, and the Allied and Canadian troops facilitated the arrival of food, fuel and other aid supplies to a population in the midst of starvation. General Charles Foulkes, commander of the 1st Canadian Corps, accepted the surrender of German forces in the Netherlands on 5 May. Two days later, Germany formally surrendered and the war in Europe came to an end.

Field Marshal Montgomery accepted and witnessed General Kienzl sign the surrender of the German land, sea and air forces in Northern Germany, Holland and Denmark.

And back to Luxembourg where the adventures of Oberleutnant Anton Heidelberg began. Most of Luxembourg was rapidly liberated in September 1944 when the front line stabilized behind the Our and Sauer Rivers along the Luxembourg-German frontier. Following the campaign in Brittany, the U.S. VIII Corps occupied the sector of the front line in Luxembourg. On 16 December 1944, elements of the U.S. 28th and 4th Infantry Divisions, as well as a combat command of the 9th Armoured Division were defending the line of the Our and Sauer Rivers when the German offensive started.

German Volksgrenadier in Luxembourg, December 1944

The initial defensive efforts of the U.S. troops hinged upon holding towns near the international frontier. As a result, some of the towns including towns Clervaux, Marnach, Holzthum, Consthum, Weiler, and Wahlhausen were used as strongholds by the Americans and attacked by the Germans, who wanted to achieve control of the road networks in northern Luxembourg for their forces to move westward. After the Americans in northern Luxembourg were forced to retreat by the German attacks, the area experienced a second passage of the front-line during January and February 1945, this time moving generally eastward as the U.S. Third Army attacked into the southern flank of the German penetration (the "Bulge"). But it wasn't until 12 February 1945 that Vianden was the final community in Luxembourg to be liberated.

As previously highlighted an agreement between the exiled Luxembourg Government and the USA, the transmitter, which had been damaged by the German army, is made available to the Psychological Warfare Division (PWD) of SHAEF (Supreme Headquarters Allied Expeditionary Forces). undermine German soldiers' morale.

The stark reality of poverty in Britain after the war when I was born on the 3 December 1945 when I was put up for adoption by my birth mother Betty Gitsham. Below is cash totalling 15/1d (fifteen shillings and one penny) in today's money 75p that my adopted parents Ada and John Slaughter paid for a week's rent for a two up two down end town-house, with a garden in Leicester in 1945

And my dad was paid just £6.00 a week as a bricklayer. During the war, classed as a reserved occupation employee, he travelled all over the country to rebuild bombed out government buildings and spent six weeks in Coventry to dig out bodies when that city was blitzed by the Luftwaffe. We were so poor that my dad would enter boxing tournaments in return for a fee of 2/6d (two shillings and six pence) and the chance of winning a fiver for a knock-out. He never won that five-pound note. His weekly builders wage was £6.00. Living next to a railway line we would clamber up the "rally-bank" to pick up the coal which had tumbled out of the tender. On occasion when the train was going past slowly the fireman would throw us a shovel full.

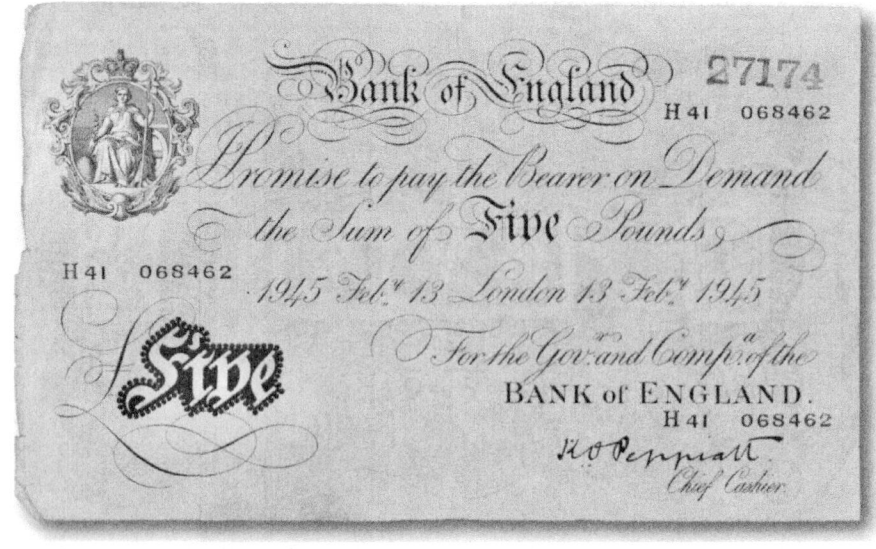

World War II ended with the unconditional surrender of Germany in May 1945, but both May 8 and May 9 are celebrated as Victory in Europe Day (or VE Day). This double celebration occurs because the Germans surrendered to the Western Allies, including Britain and the U.S. on 8 May, and a separate surrender took place on 9 May in Russia. In the East, the war ended when Japan surrendered unconditionally on 14 August 1945, signing their surrender on 2 September. The Japanese surrender occurred after the United States dropped atomic bombs on Hiroshima and Nagasaki on 6 and 9 August respectively. The date of the Japanese surrender is known as Victory Over Japan Day, or VJ Day.

On 8 May 1945, tens of thousands of people took to the streets of London to celebrate Victory in Europe Day. This momentous occasion marked the formal acceptance of Nazi Germany's unconditional surrender after nearly six years of war. At 3:00pm , Prime Minister Winston Churchill announced on the radio that the war in Europe had come to an end, following Germany's surrender the day before. The city erupted in joy and relief as people rejoiced in the streets, expressing their gratitude to the servicemen and women who had sacrificed so much during the war.

Princess Elizabeth, The Queen Mother, Winston Churchill, King George VI and Princess Margaret appear on the balcony of Buckingham Palace

During a very rare personal interview with the BBC in 1985, The Queen recalled the day she famously left the palace gates with her sister Margaret for the wild evening of celebrations – she called it "one of the most memorable nights of my life".

This was the only time the Queen has ever gone incognito among her subjects. The two princesses, aged just 19 and 14, were given permission by their father, King George VI, to join the crowds in London to celebrate VE Day for themselves and what was to follow was a remarkable series of events. London, was of course, erupting. It had been more than five long years since war broke out and the nation was gearing up for a celebration like no other. The Queen's cousin, The Hon Margaret Rhodes, and former lady-in-waiting, Jean Woodroffe, accompanied the princesses.

That night, around 8pm, Princess Elizabeth and Princess Margaret asked their parents if they could join the festivities outside. There was, naturally, some resistance – a fear for their safety, but their parents agreed if they were accompanied by a group of 16 highly trustworthy members of the royal household.

The Queen's cousin, Margaret Rhodes said, "We crossed the forecourt at Buckingham Palace and got to the railings and there were these masses and masses of people.

There was a general thing of, 'We want the King and Queen', which we all frantically joined in with and were amazed when, 5 or 10 minutes later, the windows opened, and they came out onto the balcony."

Margaret Rose continued "It was like a wonderful escape for the girls. I don't think they'd ever been out among millions of people. It was just freedom – to be an ordinary person. I don't remember who came up with the idea. We went out of one of the back doors of Buckingham Palace and headed up to the left of the Mall. There were lots of people singing and shouting".

The Queen said of the evening in her BBC interview, "We were terrified of being recognised – so I pulled my uniform cap well down over my eyes. A Grenadier officer among our party of about 16 people said he refused to be seen in the company of another officer improperly dressed. So, I had to put my cap on normally."

Lady Trumpington remembered "We rushed to the centre of London. There was Humphrey Lyttleton, blowing his trumpet like mad on the back of a lorry. I had a friend who was a bodyguard of the Queen, so I noticed her and Princess Margaret as they walked the streets of London. But they were people like anyone else – we didn't take any notice of them". The party moved to Whitehall and the Queen recalled, 'lines of people linking arms and walking down Whitehall, all of us just swept along on a tide of happiness. I also remember when someone exchanged hats with a Dutch sailor; the poor man coming along with us to get his hat back."

Winston Churchill, centre, waves to crowds gathered in front of Whitehall in London.

At around 11.30pm Margaret Rhodes said the group arrived at one of London's most famous hotels. "For some reason, we decided to go in the front door of the Ritz and do the conga. The Ritz has always been so stuffy and formal – we rather electrified the stuffy individuals inside. I don't think people realised who was among the party – I think they thought it was just a group of drunk young people. I remember old ladies looking faintly shocked. As one congaed through, eyebrows were raised".

Princesses Elizabeth and Margaret ended up in the Royal Parks on their way back to the palace. Jean Woodroffe said, "There were places like Green Park and St James's which one would never have walked through at night in the war – and there we were. There was the usual thing of people kissing and hugging and even making love. I was shocked by it! They hadn't experienced that sort of thing happening before in public".

Meanwhile in Luxembourg when the entire country was totally liberated on 12 February the Luxembourg radio transmitter, which had been damaged by the German army, was made available to an Anglo-American organisation that used radio broadcasting to undermine German soldiers' morale.

US soldiers at the Radio Luxembourg studios during WW2.

With regular English language programmes returning to the airwaves in six months' time Stephen Williams returned to Radio Luxembourg on 7 January as Director of English programmes, English-sponsored programmes start 1 July 1946.

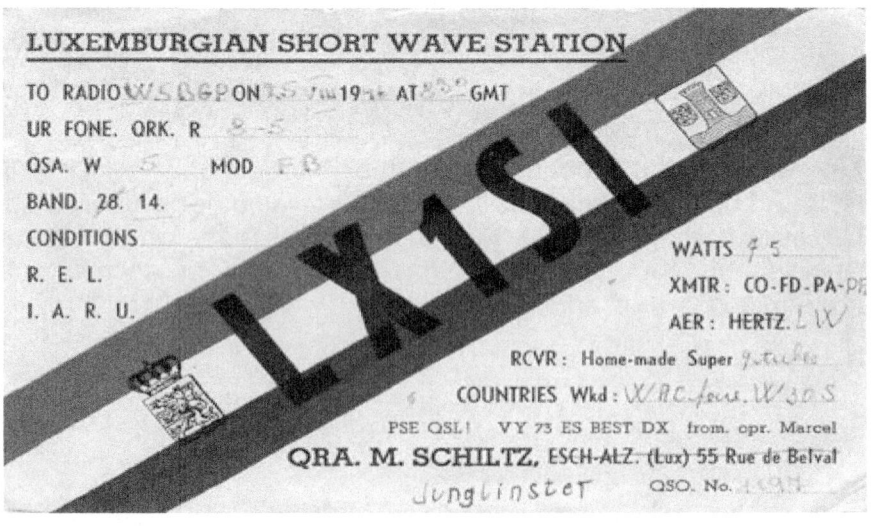

QSL card issued on 10 July 1946 indicated that audiences were listening in the United States of America.

CHAPTER FIFTEEN

ANTHONY RETURNS TO NOTTINGHAM

Having been a skilled compositor, printer and salesperson, it was not difficult for Anthony to secure a reliable position in 1956 at Millwards, one of the county's leading bespoke letter-press printing companies.

Roger Millward & Sons, a notable printing company, left an indelible mark on Nottingham's history. Thomas Forman, the founder, embarked on his printing journey in Nottingham in 1848. He acquired a printing works at 14 Long Row, where newspaper and book production formed the core of the business.

The Nottingham Daily Guardian launched in 1861 was followed by the Nottingham Evening Post in 1878, where Anthony had worked prior to WW II. As the business expanded, the original premises on Long Row became insufficient.

In 1919, the partnership dissolved, and a purpose-built printing and publishing facility emerged on Hucknall Road. Designed by celebrated architect Cecil Howitt, this new home also housed a hight-end bespoke print business, which thrived under the leadership of James Forman and his son Dudley Perry Forman.

The company's success spanned over 152 years, during which it printed millions of labels, cartons, calendars, stationery, and security items. Each division had its own sales force, and at its peak, Thomas Forman expanded his sales offices to include London, Liverpool, and Birmingham. The business also maintained its design studio, composing, reproduction, finishing, laboratory, engineering, and personnel departments.

Tragically, Mr. Dudley passed away in a riding accident at the age of 43. In 1926, the firm moved into its new headquarters on Hucknall Road. Although the factory at the rear was demolished to make way for housing, the legacy of Roger Millward & Sons endures in Nottingham's collective memory.

Their contribution to Nottingham city's printing industry remains a testament to innovation, craftsmanship and resilience.

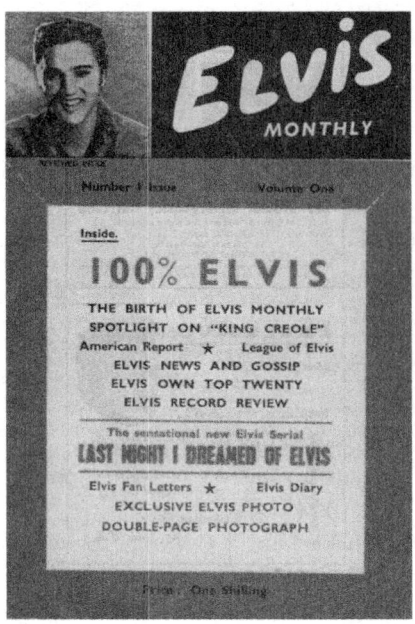

It was during his time at Millward's that Anthony was introduced to Albert Hand, a very small Derbyshire printer who in 1959 had published a couple of Elvis fanzines, "A Century of Elvis" and "The Elvis They Dig", which were sold only on mail order through small ads in the pop music press. He made enough to produce the first edition of "Elvis Monthly", which again was only available by post.

A local Nottingham newsagent Peter Keegan was asked by a customer if he could get copies of future editions through his shop, so Keegan went to find Albert. Being the Midland's boss of the magazine wholesaler Surridge Dawson he was able to get future editions on the "Monthly" into shops on the condition that it was more professionally written, produced, and printed on much better coated paper stock. Into the frame comes Anthony from Roger Millward and Sons, and a revamp led to the title selling upwards of 100,000 copies a month. This success attracted the attention of Australian entrepreneur Roger Stigwood, who later went on to manage the Bee Gees.

On arrival in England, Stigwood got a job in an institution for "wayward" teenage boys in Frinton-on-Sea but, finding this work very unpleasant, decided to open a theatrical agency, which in 1960 signed up a young actor called John Leyton also from Frinton. As acting jobs were sparse, Stigwood sent John to "singing" auditions instead. John received a series of rejections until the pop producer Joe Meek stepped in, declaring that Leyton's lack of vocal ability was no problem, as he was so good looking. Leyton was cast as a pop singer in the TV series "Harpers West One", and a song he sang on the show, "Johnny Remember Me", produced by Meek, topped the UK charts in August 1961. This success established Stigwood and Meek as Britain's first independent record producers and Stigwood became Leyton's personal manager.

While Leyton was soon more in demand as an actor, Stigwood persevered with other singers including Albert Hand's Dave Kaye and The Dykons, scoring small hits while Stigwood continued making large sums as an agent and promoter as well as part owner of Albert's Pop Weekly magazine, plus a 50% shareholder in Printhouse Limited in Eastwood, Nottingham, of which Anthony was now the Managing Director.

Stigwood began living a life of extravagance and gambled heavily. Then, in 1965, his nationwide Chuck Berry Tour (with Danny La Rue as co-star) plus a week at the London Palladium failed to draw audiences and Stigwood was forced to declare bankruptcy. (In 1967, at the suggestion of Beatles manager Brian Epstein, Robert Stigwood merged his agency with Epstein's company NEMS.

Within weeks of joining NEMS he started managing the Bee Gees, a teenage vocal group who, after many years in Australia, had just returned to their native UK with hopes of a British stardom. Within months their first international single, "New York Mining Disaster 1941", had become a major British and US hit reaching the Top 20 in both markets, while "Massachusetts" reached number 1 in the UK and number 11 in the US, launching a string of Bee Gees hits that continued throughout the late 1960s and beyond.

When Brian Epstein unexpectedly died in August 1967, Stigwood was seen as a potential successor to the NEMS organisation, but The Beatles refused to work with him. As a result he left NEMS, with a "golden handshake", to form his own Robert Stigwood Organisation, bringing the Bee Gees with him. He then purchased a controlling interest in Associated London Scripts, a writers' agency co-founded by Spike Milligan and Eric Sykes in 1954, in which many of Britain's best comedy and television scriptwriters had been involved.

Robert Stigwood produced many shows "Hair" and "Oh! Calcutta!" for the West End stage in 1968 and 1970 respectively, and by 1971 he had produced the first stage production of "Jesus Christ Superstar" - initially in the USA, the beginning of a successful working relationship with Andrew Lloyd Webber and Tim Rice which continued later in the decade with "Evita".

Bob Stigwood urged the Bee Gees to change their sound from the ballads which had made them famous, and to move towards the disco sound that would bring them their greatest success, starting with "Jive Talking" a US Billboard chart topper in 1975. The records were released on Stigwood's own label, RSO Records, which he founded in 1973.Stigwood expanded into film production with success. His first feature film was a hit screen adaptation of Tim and Andrew's "Jesus Christ Superstar" (1973), made in association with its director, Norman Jewison. He followed this with the film version of The Who's "Tommy" (1975), which became one of the most successful films at the box office during its year of release.

Surprisingly he signed actor John Travolta to a million dollar three-picture contract in 1976. Many in the film industry were reportedly sceptical, because Travolta was at that time was only known as a TV actor; but RSO Films' next production, "Saturday Night Fever", made him a leading movie star. The film had an unlikely source - a supposedly factual magazine article which Stigwood had licensed. The double-LP soundtrack, written by and featuring the Bee Gees, became the biggest selling soundtrack album ever released. Stigwood followed this with a hugely successful film adaptation of the stage rock'n'roll musical "Grease" (1978), which co-starred Travolta and Australian singer Olivia Newton-

John. Stigwood insisted that additional songs be added to the soundtrack, including the theme tune penned by Barry Gibb and songs by fellow Australian songwriter-producer John Farrar. Gibb and Robert Stigwood's production partner Allan Carr convinced Stigwood to bring Frankie Valli in to sing the title track.

The amount of pop music titles produced by the Hand/Stigwood organisation was outstanding for a small back street publisher in Heanor, and all printed by Anthony's company Printhouse Limited.

Each title enjoyed an affinity with Radio Luxembourg, and later in the great scheme included CLUB 208 a listeners affinity title to the iconic broadcaster which took 1,000s of British radio fans to meet the DJs and see the transmitters and studios.

Outselling all these titles was the 1962 title "Pop Weekly" which being printed on coated paper was more collectable that the newspaper print versions of the NME, Disc, Record Mirror and Melody Maker. And each title enjoyed a Christmas Annual published by World Distributors each selling 100,000 copies.

(Above: Picture Still from the film "Elvis That's The Way It Is" showing 208 DJs Tony Prince and Peter Aldersley riding Elvis' bike around the streets of Luxembourg). In 1970, upon the instruction

of Presley's manager Colonel Tom Parker, MGM flew over a film crew to the Grand Duchy for an international Elvis Festival held in the New Theatre – footage of the event was included in the movie "Elvis That's The Way It Is" with 600 Elvis fans from the UK joining up with members from all over Europe.In 1972, the Elvis Fan Club started to operate trips to see Elvis in Las Vegas supported by 208 Tony Prince introduced Elvis from the Hilton stage referring to his station Radio Luxembourg. After the show he was mobbed by former GIs based in Germany who chose 208 in preference to their American Forces Network. Over the years it was Luxembourg DJs who visited Elvis never anyone at that time from the BBC and including Savile, Peter Aldersley, Tony Prince, Rosko (his dad made Elvis movies for MGM) Don Wardell and Mark Wesley. Picture left: Elvis on stage in Las Vegas in 1968 receiving his Radio Luxembourg "Battle of the Giants" trophy.

Also, in the 1970s Radio Luxembourg listeners were invited to join "Club 208" which had its own request show and monthly magazine. The club magazine printed by Anthony and operated and edited by Todd Slaughter attracted 100s of members to travel to Luxembourg on organised holidays to meet the DJs and see the studios and the transmitters. (Peter Powell with Todd meeting coaches of Club 208 fans – below).

Radio Luxembourg and the population of the Grand Duchy was important to all of Europe before, during and after the war. People in Luxembourg helped Anthony and in return he helped them. There is no other radio station anywhere in the world that has such an amazing history, and it should be remembered. In a few years those millions of

devoted listeners, and hundreds of music performers plus unique radio personalities will no longer be around to remember just how much of a powerful influence 208 was around the world. Many overseas listeners honed their English skills by listening to the English language service of Radio Télé Luxembourg. (More about Club 208 later.)

BACKGROUNDER:
From its inception in 1933 the international services of Radio Luxembourg brought commercial radio to many European countries including Great Britain. With millions of listeners, it was lost in the ether during the war years except for the various propaganda broadcasts provided by the German occupiers of the country and the studios. The arrival of pirate radio operating around the UK coast from ships anchored in international waters and aboard former WW II artillery forts saw the first blow to its audience figures providing 24 hours a day pop radio. The Marine Offences bill passed by the UK parliament prohibiting UK persons broadcasting, supplying, and selling advertising closed all but Radio Caroline. The new clear local commercial independent land-based radio stations delivered a

knockout blow to the continental giant and the high-powered AM service on 208 meters on the medium wave band was proving too costly to operate.

In 1989, hoping to build a new audience, Luxembourg in English once more returned with a daytime schedule for the first time since the early 1950s, but this time it was not aimed at the Brits but to a non-commercial Scandinavian audience.

Using a 24 hour stereo transponder on the Astra 1A satellite to supplement the 208 analogue night-time service it enjoyed a fantastic outreach.

The end, however, eventually came for 208's AM service at 3am GMT on 30 December 1991 (the station did return to the analogue 208/1440 for one night a year later when the station finally closed its digital service), the last record played on AM being Van Morrison's "In the Days Before Rock and Roll" (chosen mainly because of its mention of the radio station in the lyrics).

"At the End of the Day" (one of their closedown songs) which was played heading into the top of the hour (even though DJ Jeff Graham had said that they were going to play the original closedown tune, it was not in fact the original song, but a later version the station used as the original was not located, "It's Time To Say Goodnight").

The station then went onto satellite and shortwave (15350 kHz) only, with the first songs played being "When Will You (Make My Telephone Ring)" by Deacon Blue and "Always" by Atlantic Starr.

The satellite and shortwave service continued until midnight on 30 December 1992. The closedown night was relayed on various stations, including the old 208 wavelength. The Van Morrison song again was the next-to-last record that night, followed by Marion Montgomery's "Maybe the Morning".

CHAPTER SIXTEEN

THE NIGHT HAS A THOUSAND SPIES

An unassuming printer would never expect to be in the company of rock stars, actors and show business impresarios but producing some of the UK's most popular music titles gave Anthony VIP "access all areas" opportunities. Although Albert Hand was credited as being the editor of all his titles much of the journalistic content was created by Anthony and writer David Cardwell.

David was the co-founder and executive chairman of the brand licensing company Copyright Promotions Limited (CPL, now CPLG). David and his business partner, Richard Culley, were among those who established the UK licensing industry, thus shaping a significant sector of British business, and building on the childhood memories of generations.

David recognised the powerful appeal of treasured children's characters and realised their potential to reach beyond their original story contexts. Across Europe, CPL was responsible for toys, clothing, food, and other items inspired by and adorned with beloved characters including Noddy, the Mr Men and Little Miss, Dangermouse, Tom and Jerry, the Pink Panther, the Teenage Mutant Hero Turtles, the Flintstones and My Little Pony, and imagery from cartoon and film series such as Thunderbirds, Spiderman, X-Men, Star Trek and Star Wars.

David was born in the village of Huntspill in Somerset, the son of Thomas Cardwell, a steel fixer, and Marie (nee Raven), a school cook. He left school at 14 and travelled to London with no money or academic qualifications, but full of ideas, energy, and ambition. He started out as an errand boy for the Daily Express; helped Albert Hand create the Elvis Monthly magazine; worked as a music journalist, including for NME and Pop Weekly; and became a publicist and manager for new pop music acts, most notably the Paper Dolls and Pikkettywitch. In 1974 David co-founded CPL and began work, with the Cosgrove Hall animation studio, on a TV series of Noddy.

Anthony also picked up a great deal of celebrity printing contracts because of his business dealings with David Cardwell, Joe Meek, Robert Stigwood, Micky Most and Ashley Kozak, was a British jazz bassist, record producer and artists' manager, best known as having been Donovan's manager. He told the story often that he was delivering printing to Ashley's home and from outside he could hear that there was a party going down. The door opened and there was the Scottish folk singer with a naked girl on his shoulders. Anthony's most infamous clients were MP John Profumo and Doctor Steven Ward.

It all began by the swimming pool at Cliveden July 1961. John Profumo, who was the front bench minister of war in Harold Macmillan's Conservative government was a weekend guest in the main house of Lord Astor.

John Profumo and "Doctor" Stephen Ward co-conspirators in the nation's sex & spy scandal

Christine Keeler and Mandy Rice Davies were also staying for the weekend in the grounds, at Spring Cottage, on the banks of the Thames, as the guests of Lord Astor's tenant Stephen Ward. John Profumo and Christine met by chance at the poolside and soon afterwards began an affair. In January 1963, she said that Stephen Ward had told her to ask Profumo when the US would share atomic secrets with West Germany. She also admitted that at the time of her affair with Profumo she was also going to bed with Eugene

Ivanov, a naval attaché at the Soviet Russian embassy. (Below: Mandy and Christine)

In the months that followed a furious press storm was whipped up by newspapers hostile to the Macmillan government. Profumo was forced to resign from politics in June 1963. The Metropolitan Police were instructed by the home secretary to have Ward arrested on charges under the Sexual Offences Act. Witnesses were called upon to give false and damaging evidence against him. He was a victimised in a show trial in which the Lord Chief Justice made a shameful conviction and Stephen Ward took a fatal overdose while the jury was considering its verdicts.

Christine Keeler, who had been pressurised by the police into giving false evidence in a related case involving her ex-lover Aloysius "Lucky" Gordon, was subsequently imprisoned for the perjury that she had committed under police direction.

Her life, Ward's, Astor's, Profumo's, and others were ruined by the case. Its effect was to provide sex education classes on the front pages of daily newspapers throughout 1963. Sex became public and political in a way that they had never been before. Sexual intercourse began in 1963, as Philip Larkin wrote in a famous poem. He said the change came between the end of the ban on "Lady Chatterley's Lover" and **The Beatles'** first LP. It was the Profumo Affair that put sexual intercourse on the front page.

The Beatles US LP cover prior to this album's release, every Beatles long-player had featured more-or-less unremarkable photos of the four mop-topped Liverpool lads. They might have been smiling down from the steps of the EMI headquarters, depicted in various cheeky photo booth poses or staring hazily into the camera. But they were unmistakably on-brand as the clean-cut pop superstars Brian Epstein wanted them to be. Suddenly, the Yesterday and Today artwork had them practising the kind of macabre humour that would have shocked and appalled teeny-bopper fans and their parents. When Capitol Records began shipping its initial print run of 750,000 album copies out to stores, there was an immediate backlash. A huge proportion of American record stores refused to stock the record.

Capitol Records had to initiate a military-style operation to recall the album. Most already-pressed copies were replaced with a more sanitary cover image of the band posing around a luggage trunk. The idea for the "butcher" album cover came from its photographer, Robert Whitaker, who had already photographed the band on their previous American tour. John Lennon later described to Radio Luxembourg listeners that Whitaker was "a bit of a surrealist" who brought the dolls and pieces of meat to a photo shoot without prior warning.

Having become sick of photo sessions because, in Lennon's words, the band "had to try and look normal and...didn't feel it", The Beatles loved the bizarre idea. Paul McCartney supposedly told the record company it was their "comment" on the mass slaughter of the Vietnam War. At the time, anti-war sentiment was rising among Britain and American youth. This swell of a counter cultural feeling was beginning to reflect itself in the ideas of bands like The Beatles. Of course, gory surrealism and opposition to a government-sanctioned war were never going to wash with major record store chains. And so, this album cover was destined to make censorship history.

CHAPTER SEVENTEEN

ALBERT HAND DEAD – LONG LIVE THE KING

Albert Hand (pictured with Elvis) , the founder of "Elvis Monthly" died 18 April 1972 twelve years after the title first hit the bookstalls. By 1972 all the other Albert Hand Publications which were printed and created by Anthony had folded. Elvis Monthly continued for a further 28 years edited by me Todd Slaughter. Albert had lost interest in his pop publishing business in 1970 with Anthony selecting content and writing editorials in Albert's name, and after his passing under the signature of his wife Phyllis for a further eighteen months. (Albert pictured with Elvis in Idyllwild California during filming of "Wild in the Country". He gave Elvis three leather bound books.

One contained the names and addresses of the magazines' readers thanking him, one contained all the nice things the fans had written about Elvis and the third book contained all of Elvis' activities during his career to date). With Pop Weekly, Mod's Monthly, Teenbeat, Record Collector, Pop Ten Monthly, and Fury Monthly all folding the business was on the skids. During its heyday this back street publishing empire and associated records-by-mail operation was colossal, but where had all the money gone? Having purchased the brand, "The Official Elvis Presley Fan Club" for £2,000 (paid for in instalments). Come 1973 I was asked by one of his partners to take control of Heanor Record Centre Limited. Anthony helped me restructure an ailing operation which had no assets and was trading insolvently. Publishing was a way forward and with tens of thousands of Elvis photographs in the building we produced a series of Presley commemoratives, which following Elvis' death catapulted in circulation We also published industry titles Pump News, Rock Video, and CB News together with a spin off comic 10-4 Action.

In 1980 I was in Atlanta for the launch on CNN, and six weeks later in Las Vegas with Elvis' former manager Colonel Tom Parker I attended a Satellite Industry conference and exhibition. We published Satellite TV News – the UK's first pre Sky communication periodical in 1982, selling it to "Spotlight Magazines, a division of the Daily Express group which was then retitled "Satellite and Cable TV News". It operated for a few years, but due to a lack of advertising revenue it ceased publication a matter of weeks before Rupert Murdoch held a press conference to announce that he was going to launch the world's first domestic direct from satellite broadcast TV service using the Luxembourg owned Astra Satellite.

THE SES DISH FARM LOCATED IN BETZDORF IN EASTERN LUXEMBOURG

Astra was the brand name for SES geostationary communication satellites, both individually and as a group, which are owned and operated by SES S.A., a global satellite operator based in Betzdorf, in eastern Luxembourg. The name is also used to describe the pan-European broadcasting system provided by these satellites, the channels carried on them, and even the reception equipment. At the time of the launch of the first Astra satellite, Astra 1A in 1988, the satellite's operator was known as Société Européenne des Satellites ("European Satellite Company"). In 2001 SES Astra, a newly formed subsidiary of SES, operated the Astra satellites and in September 2011, SES Astra was consolidated back into the parent company, which by this time also operated other satellite families such as AMC, and NSS.

Today Astra satellites broadcast 2,600 digital television channels (675 in high definition) via five main satellite orbital position to 300 million homes across the UK, Europe and around the world.

Meanwhile back in Blighty other pop media fanzines from Anthony and myself followed including Cliff With The Kids in America, Rastamag, Cannon & Ball, Club 208 Magazine, and John Lennon – A Tribute. As revolutionary as many of these magazines were,

the Elvis connection of the business was legendary. And as such Anthony and I were asked to attend a meeting with 208 boss Alan Keen (left) at the Radio Luxembourg offices at 38 Hertford Street in Mayfair, London W1 in June 1973.

In 1964 Alan Keen was working for the Daily Mirror Group, selling advertising space in its newspapers and magazines. It had been his job for the previous sixteen years - twelve of them with the Mirror - and before that he had been involved with parliamentary reporting and spent time in the RAF. One day he got back to his office to be told that a man he didn't know called Philip Birch, who worked for the advertising agency J. Walter Thompson, had been trying to get in touch with him. Alan called Philip back and they agreed to meet - but not at the agency. They had a secret rendezvous at the Hilton Hotel on London's Park Lane. Birch told him he was about to leave JWT to launch an offshore radio station. Radio Caroline and a couple of smaller operations already existed but Birch told him this one was going to be bigger and better than any of them. And he offered Alan a job as a sales executive. He took a while to think about it, discussed it with his wife and, despite her reservations, decided that it might be fun. In August 1964 Alan joined Radlon Sales Ltd., the sales arm of the new station, which was to be called Radio London. At that time there was just Managing Director Philip Birch and Secretary Margaret Greville in the office with him, but they were soon joined by Dennis Maitland, Roger Seddon, Eddie Blackwell, Godfrey Morrow, who always wore exquisite shoes, and Desmond Brown. They were an experienced sales team with plenty of industry connections and, despite Radio London still being some months away from commencing broadcasts, they were able to pre-sell some £100,000 of airtime before it launched. The first advert was for the News of the World newspaper. Radio London was an instant success.

The tightly formatted programmes, the slick disc-jockeys, the American jingles and the strong signal meant that it very quickly became the most popular offshore station in the country. And behind the scenes it was probably the most efficiently run and professional operation too. All was going well until the then Labour government headed by Prime Minister Harold Wilson made it illegal for the station to carry British companies' advertisements. At 3pm on 14 August 1967 Radio London closed. An emotional time for the listeners, it was also traumatic for the people who worked for the station. On 1 August 1970 Alan returned to broadcasting when he joined the English service of Radio Luxembourg as General Manager, later becoming its Managing Director. The station had already started cutting back on the sponsored programmes. Alan was determined to continue this process and make as much of the output live from the Grand Duchy as possible. With a team of excellent DJs, many of them ex-pirates, it was a golden era for Radio Luxembourg. Alan Keen played a major part in UK broadcasting from 1964 to 1980, as a senior figure two of the country's finest music radio stations; Radio London (at sea) and Radio Luxembourg (West Europe) He died in April 2019, aged 91.

Alan Keen was very much aware that 6 years after the "pirates" were sunk commercial radio was coming to the UK. LBC news radio was due to launch on 8 October 1973, with Capital Radio – the first pop music service – a week later. He was also impressed whilst somewhat amazed that a small publishing operation in the old mining town of Heanor in Derbyshire, through its titles, had generated an extraordinary amount of national and international publicity to Radio Luxembourg. In 1970 the broadcaster's brand was featured on screen on the MGM movie "Elvis: That's the Way It Is." Picture below Dave Kaye & The Dykons performing for an eager Elvis audience.

It was an even bigger surprise to Alan, and the Luxembourg government that the MGM company had not only sent over to the Grand Duchy a full camera crew and technicians from their studios in Culver City, California but one of their top producers, Dennis Sanders who was an American film director, screenwriter and producer who directed the debut performances of Robert Redford and Tom Skerritt in the 1962 film War Hunt.

He won two Academy Awards, the first for Best Short Subject in 1955 for A Time Out of War that had served as his master's degree thesis at UCLA and which he co-scripted with his brother Terry Sanders; and the second for Best Documentary in 1970 for Czechoslovakia 1968.

In 1958, he teamed up again with Terry Sanders to adapt Norman Mailer's World War II novel The Naked and the Dead. He was born in New York City, the son of sculptor and designer Altina Schinasi. He died from a heart attack on 10 December 1987 in San Diego, California, age just 58, where he was professor and film maker in residence at San Diego State University.

It was Elvis' manager and his appreciation of the publicity that his star had enjoyed via our operation across Europe that he insisted that MGM should go to Luxembourg and record our event for his latest Elvis MGM movie.

And when Colonel Parker makes such demands then even those with the ultimate power jumped to attention. For Alan Keen to team up with Anthony and myself was a no-brainer.

Alan's idea was for our company to launch a Radio Luxembourg listeners' club featuring their radio stars and giving the most devoted the opportunity to meet the DJs. It was to be a three-year contract which was t operated in association with the recently formed Daily Mirror Pop Club, and Fabulous 208.

First published as Fabulous on 18 January 1964. Fleetway Publications had seen the popularity of our Pop Weekly a glossy magazine selling 100,000 copies each week, and like us had judged the competition - chiefly the NME and Melody Maker – as being non-cherished newsprint publications.

Dennis Sanders in Luxembourg

Fleetway wanted our market share and more. As Paul Jobling and David Crowley note, the Beatles went on to appear in every edition of the magazine for the next two years, and several early editions featured no other artists.

By June 1966, when Fleetway had become part of IPC, after a deal with Radio Luxembourg to carry its programme listings and related items, the magazine was retitled " Fabulous 208": *Two Oh Eight* being Luxy's AM frequency.

At its peak it was selling a quarter of a million copies, and for the majority of the 1960s had the biggest market share of its type, which accelerated the closure of Pop Weekly.

Elvis Monthly in the meantime continued to flourish – there was even a French language edition "Elvis Mensuel" translated by Anthony and compiled by Marie du Bois de Vroylande who during WWII used the attic of her Brussels apartment as a hideaway for downed British airman, deserters and Jewish escapees. Marie was also the cookery editor of "Femmes d'Aujourd'hui" which was first published on 1 April 1933 and being the only Belgian women's magazine. Its founder was an entrepreneur, Jan Meuwissen, and it was published by s.a. Femmes d'Aujourd'hui. The magazine was part of a company owned by Jan Meuwissen. Published in Belgium it has a circulation at its height of one and a half million copies across Belgium France and Switzerland.

CLUB 208 magazine was to be a fanzine, published for members only with trips to Luxembourg, just as we were taking Elvis fans into Europe and across the USA.

It was an interesting time for everyone both in the London office and in the Radio Luxembourg studios in the Grand Duchy. British celebrities on tour across Europe would make the effort to travel to the Grand Duchy to meet the DJs in their place of work and some of the biggest acts included Queen, David Bowie and Led Zeppelin. In London every domestic and recording artists visiting the UK would beat a path to their Hertford Street studios. Frank Sinatra, The Beatles, Stones, Tom Jones, Cliff Richard, The Osmonds, David Cassidy, Petula Clark, Dusty Springfield, Cilla Black, and Shirley Bassey. Some even hosted their own programmes on 208. In addition to the monthly fanzines there were also special events editions printed by Anthony including Rodney Collins (Publicity Director 208) paperback book "Radio Luxembourg 1979", published 1 January 1978.

Rodney Collins, who lives in Yorkshire, started out on the music paper Record Mirror in the late 60's, before working for the ATV

Theatres Division and the ATV -Pye Records and then joining BBC Radio 1 and 2 in the early 70's. He moved to Radio Luxembourg as Director of News Programming in the mid 70's and then on as Managing Director of local radio stations in London and Scotland. In 2000 he set up his own syndicated radio business and the show on Sine FM - Soundtrack of Your Life - is exactly that....listeners send in requests and details of music that meant so much to them in earlier years.

And then there was a daytime Radio Luxembourg service branded as Atlantic 252 which was an Irish longwave radio station broadcasting to Ireland and the United Kingdom on 252 kHz (1190 metres) from its 1988 purpose-built transmission site at Clarkstown radio transmitter, County Meath, which provided service to Atlantic 252 from 1989 until 2002.

The station's studios were located 7 miles away in Mornington House, Summerhill Road, Trim, County Meath. Atlantic 252 also had sales offices and studios at 74 Newman Street in London.

The concept of Atlantic 252 can be traced to as far back as August 1986, when broadcaster RTÉ announced it was to use its allocated longwave frequency for a new pop music station. Ireland (and RTE) had been allocated a long wave frequency at the Regional Administrative Radio Broadcasting Conference in Geneva in 1975. RTÉ teamed up with RTL Group / Radio Luxembourg to form Radio Tara – the trading name of Atlantic 252 – which, being on long wave, was able to provide reception across Ireland and the United Kingdom. The Irish Government allowed RTE to allocate their 252 licence to Radio Tara. The broadcaster Pat Kenny, who was a member of the RTE Board was Chairman of Radio Tara (Atlantic 252) between 1990 and 1992. This followed Spangles Muldoon/Chris Cary's pirate Radio XIDY test transmissions on 254 kHz longwave in the mid-1980s.

The Radio Tara company was officially registered in 1985, with trading names of Radio Tara, Atlantic 252 and Tara 254, it was dissolved in 2011.

In 1987, RTÉ commenced building a giant three-sided 248 metre broadcast radio tower mast in County Meath, using a specially built pair of air- and water-cooled high energy 300 kW solid-state transmitters (which could be combined to give double power) built by the Varian Associates Inc. Texas, company despite protests from local residents. Studios were set up in Mornington House, in the nearby town of Trim. The station cost £6 million to set up. Just over 47 million people were in the station's broadcast reception area.

At 8.00am local time on the morning of 1 September 1989 Gary King announced on Atlantic 252, "Mine is the first voice you will ever hear on Atlantic 252".

The station's official "first record ever played" – on the launch date of 1 September 1989 – was "Sowing the Seeds of Love" by Tears for Fears, followed by "Monkey" by George Michael. The first record played during the period of Atlantic 252's test transmissions had been "Ain't Nobody" by Rufus and Chaka Khan ('89 Remix).

This was followed by a specially produced pre-recorded introduction tape that introduced everybody employed by the radio station on its launch day, from engineers, administration, management like Travis Baxter and John Catlett, and the station's personality music presenter line-up, including ex-Laser 558 presenter Charlie Wolf, Henry Owens, Mary Ellen O'Brien, Dusty Rhodes, Al Dunne, Tony West, Jeff Graham and the station's Laser Hot Hits and former BBC newsreader Andrew Turner. An appearance was even made by Rosalyn Reilly, who was to remain the station's cleaning lady for its entire twelve-year history.

Although the transmitter was in Ireland, the signal's reach meant that it was often looked upon as a "UK national station". Reception reports were received from all over Europe and from as far afield as Berlin, Finland, Ibiza, Canada, USA and Moscow. The signal had even been received in Brazil at night-time. The Scottish musician Mylo has claimed that it was the only station with listenable reception on the Isle of Skye. At launch there were no UK-wide commercial stations (the first would be Classic FM in 1992), and the lack of a UK broadcast licence attracted the attention of the IBA. Although the transmitters were theoretically capable of being combined to operate at a radiated power of 600 kW, international agreements limited it to a daytime maximum 500 kW, and just 100 kW during the hours of darkness.

The station transmitted only from 6a.m. until 7p.m., outside of which listeners were invited to tune to Radio Luxembourg. In August 1990, the station extended its broadcasting hours to 2a.m. with post-midnight output being automated under the branding of The Big Mattress. In September 1991, Atlantic 252 began broadcasting a 24-hour service, although until the middle of the decade, overnight programming continued to be automated.

Enda Caldwell is an Irish radio personality and voice actor. As of 2022, he was the "drivetime host" at New York's EDM station, Pulse 87. Caldwell has also worked at radio stations elsewhere in the world, including Tony Prince's United DJ Radio and the global Radio Luxembourg Digital RL station Riviera Radio, Today FM and Atlantic 252.

The Atlantic 252 music format consisted of high-rotation mainstream pop and rock music, with influences borrowed heavily from American radio, and through to 1993, a lot of the station's music was drawn from the top part of the US charts. The station mixed the best songs from the last few years along with the best songs from the top 40 – this was called "Today's Best Music Variety".

News summaries were broadcast at 10 to and 20 past the hour during the breakfast show and during part of the drive time show. RTL Commercial Radio and the BBC initially objected to the station, as they did with 208 saying that it was once again just another commercial pirate. However, as UK commercial radio developed and deregulation saw many more stations launching, formats similar to Atlantic's began to appear on FM and Atlantic

252's audience began to decline. Attempts at repositioning followed, including "Real Music, Real Radio", when the station attempted to tackle BBC Radio 1's "new music" format. At the peak of its popularity in 1993, Atlantic 252 had six million listeners aged 15+ in the UK and Ireland, but vastly increased competition from local radio stations with similar formats saw this decline.

The last show on Atlantic was presented by Enda Caldwell on 20 December 2001. This was followed by a tribute show produced by Enda Caldwell and Eric Murphy celebrating the station's twelve-year history of broadcasting and featuring classic airchecks of each year of Atlantic 252's history. The station then transitioned to automation, and continued broadcasting music without continuity, along with pre-booked commercials, until midnight on 2 January 2002, when transmissions ceased.

Many of the original line-up came from the radio ship Laser 558, UK Commercial Radio, BBC Radio One and the Irish presenters came from Dublin Super Pirates like Sunshine 101 and SuperQ 102. During the early years the presenters that worked utilised funny names, an idea originated in the US at stations like WHTZ FM Z100. Notable presenters included: Bam Bam, Robin Banks, Sandy Beach, Enda Caldwell, David Dunne, Rick O'Shea, Eddy Temple-Morris, Charlie Wolf, and Tony Wrighton.

The Radio Luxembourg association with Atlantic 252 was not often mentioned on-air, but its legacy is still celebrated with new discoveries, and past personalities.

My 30-year search for World War Two hero

His own story by Alan Bailey

CLEARING the shelves of dusty old 78rpm records was a regular chore when I worked as a sound engineer for Radio Luxembourg back in the 1960s.

The old shellac records weighed heavily on the shelves, but I didn't mind sorting through them as I occasionally came across something that appealed.

On one particular day, I'd no idea this task would lead to 30 years of searching before I could finally complete the story of a Second World War hero.

I spotted some old German recordings, which I recognised by their Reichsrundfunk label.

I knew they were Nazi broadcasts, thanks to the German I picked up from my time in the Royal Signals when I was in National Service and, as nobody wanted them, I took them home.

Crackling

A few weeks passed before I had time to listen, and the content was quite remarkable. After the typically-clipped tones of a British voice, obviously a collaborator talking about the "enemy" which would save been the British, there was a greeting sent by a captured submariner to his wife and son back home in Cornwall.

I'd no idea what had happened to this submariner POW — he could have been killed moments after making the recording, which was obviously German propaganda to show the British that Germans weren't all bad.

Initially, I didn't want to write for fear of opening up old wounds, so I tried to find out more about him through the Royal Navy.

However, it was only in May this year, I discovered I'd misheard the name.

I'd started thinking about tracing the family again. It had been bothering me for so long, I felt I had to try one more time.

Thrilled

As so many years had passed, I decided I'd write a letter to the address in Cornwall and see where it got me.

A few days later, I was thrilled to receive a reply from James's sister-in-law, Jane Berry. She wrote back, explaining not only that I had the surname wrong, and it was in fact Fulthorpe, but that James had died many years ago, and that I'd lost contact with his son so couldn't help more.

She did recall the broadcast, although the family hadn't heard it — a neighbour had come rushing round to tell them about it at the time. They were so relieved because they hadn't heard from him for so long and assumed he'd already been killed. Carlton was just four years old at the time.

Now I knew the correct name, I set about finding his address. I wrote to him at his home in Sussex, and he phoned the next day. It's the most satisfying thing I've ever done. I made him a copy and gave the original to the Royal Navy Submarine Museum at Gosport in Hampshire, as one of their staff, George Malcolmson, was so helpful.

He gave me details of how James was captured in 1943 when his submarine was depth-charged off the coast of Sicily by an Italian warship. The ill-strung crew escaped, but were machine-gunned by a German JU88 aircraft.

Prisoner

One man was killed and the rest were taken prisoner by Italians. James spent the rest of the war behind barbed wire, but received the Distinguished Service Medal when he returned.

I'll give the remaining old 78s to the Imperial War Museum in London so others can listen. People tell me I'd have made a fortune selling them, but I'm not bothered about that.

It's far more satisfying to have finally reunited a man with his late father's voice, and to give the rest of the nation an opportunity to learn about men like James Fulthorpe. It's because of people like him that we're free today.

• As told to Suzanne Roberts

Alan with two of the old Nazi records he discovered.

Paul Burnett began his radio career while in the Royal Air Force in the Persian Gulf in 1964.

In 1966 he joined Radio 270, broadcasting from a ship off Scarborough, North Yorkshire.

After the banning of the offshore stations he moved in 1967 to Manx Radio on the Isle of Man, but he soon joined Radio Luxembourg, where he hosted the chart show. Here Burnett discovered many recordings, previously thought lost, of propaganda broadcasts by William Joyce ("Lord Haw Haw") to Britain, made from the Luxembourg stations during the Nazi occupation. On Luxembourg, he presented the Saturday Top 20 show from 1967 to 1974. On 24 March 1974 Burnett joined BBC Radio 1 hosting a Sunday morning show *All There Is To Hear* (a radio one airplay chart show) and also hosted the station's national Top 20 show, broadcast on Sunday evenings between 6 and 7pm whilst Tom Browne, the main presenter of the show at the time, was absent. The first record he ever played on the station was Seven Seas Of Rhye by the group Queen. In 1976, an on-air parody of the U.S. hit single "Convoy", became "Convoy GB" (by Laurie Lingo & The Dipsticks), which led to a release of the song as a single along with fellow DJ Dave Lee Travis. The song reached 4 in the UK Singles Chart, and Paul Burnett appeared dressed as a chicken on Top of the Pops. From 5 July 1976 he hosted the weekday lunchtime show after Johnnie Walker left the station and moved to California. Here Burnett had the responsibility of revealing the new singles chart every Tuesday lunchtime on 247 metres Medium Wave as the chart positions were received by the British Market Research Bureau. His popular show included several features such as Pub of the Day, Fun at One and Is, Was, Should Have. Burnett became a regular presenter of Top of the Pops, and presented the Radio 1 Roadshow during the summer. In 1981 he moved from lunchtimes to later in the afternoons, but his daily show ended in 1982 to allow Steve Wright's show to be extended. During 1982–84, Burnett was heard on BBC Radio 2 as a stand-in host for the likes of David Hamilton and Terry Wogan and occasionally presenting the Early Show. In 1978, Burnett co-hosted the Miss World contest broadcast.

Mark Wesley, Paul Burnett, Kid Jensen, Bob Stewart, Dave Christian, and Tony Prince in the grounds of the Villa Louvigny located in the Luxembourg Municipal Park (1972)

And sponsorship opportunités were always avalable at a price

LUXEMBOURG – A PROUD NATION

The Grand Duchy of Luxembourg - a small country landlocked by Belgium, France and Germany - is a prominent financial centre. With roots stretching back to the 10th century, Luxembourg's history is closely intertwined with that of its more powerful neighbours, especially Germany. Despite declaring its neutrality, Luxembourg was occupied by Germany during both World Wars. Many of its inhabitants are trilingual in French, German and Luxembourgish. French and Luxembourgish was banned by the Nazi regime when it occupied the country during WW II.

After renewed occupation in World War II, Luxembourg abandoned its neutrality and became a front-rank enthusiast for international co-operation. Luxembourg's prosperity was formerly based on steel manufacturing. With the decline of that industry, Luxembourg diversified and is now best known for its status as Europe's most powerful investment management centre. Luxembourg exerts immense media clout and has a long tradition of operating radio and TV services for pan-European audiences, including those in France, Germany and the UK. Generations of British listeners grew up with Radio Luxembourg, which beamed pop music programmes into the UK. "The Great 208" is no more, but media group RTL is still a key player in media markets across Europe. Luxembourg's media empire extends to the skies. It is home to Europe's largest satellite operator, Societe Europeenne des Satellites (SES), which operates the Astra fleet.

The Grand Duke of Luxembourg succeeded to the title in 2000, on the abdication of his father Jean. He had already exercised the constitutional powers of the monarch since 1998. Born in 1955, the future Grand Duke Henri studied politics in Geneva, where he met his Cuban wife, Maria Teresa. He later underwent officer training at Britain's Sandhurst.

At the time of going to print Luc Frieden became Luxembourg's Prime Minister in November 2023 following six weeks of talks after the October 2023 elections, which saw his Christian Social People's Party (CSV), Luxembourg's long-dominant centre-right party, slightly increasing its vote share. The incumbent coalition led by Xavier Bettel's ruling coalition lost its majority due to a decline in support for the Greens. Frieden, a former finance minister, leads a coalition of his own Christian Social People's Party and the liberal party of former Prime Minister Xavier Bettel, who has taken over as the country's foreign minister. Luxembourg abandoned its neutrality in 1948 and forms an economic union with Belgium and the Netherlands - the Benelux countries and joins NATO. Luxembourg became founder member of the European Economic Community (now the European Union) which came into effect in January 1958.

CELEBRITY PICTURES OF THOSE VISITING THE LONDON HQ

Left to right: **Beatles outside of the 38 Hertford Street; DJ Barry Alldis with Cliff Richard; and who can forget the ubiquitous influencer Mr Horace Bachelor's K-E-Y-N-S-H-A-M**

Below:: **The entrance to the London studios of Radio Luxembourg with David Cassidy with a Hertford Street balcony appearance.**

Left to right: **Frank Sinatra in the 208 London Studios, with legendary broadcaster Pete Murray photographed outside of 38 Hertford Street.**

Show business personalities in the 208 London studios as guest on presenters shows. Top to bottom: **Harry Secombe; Paul & Ringo with Henry Cooper; Hughie Green with Bobby Vinton; Honeycombs with Jimmy Young; Adam Faith, Peter Paul and Mary with DJs Pete Murray & Alan Freeman; Matt Monroe, Cliff Richard, Joe Loss, and Roy Orbison, Shirley Bassey, Frank Ifield. Pearl Carr & Teddy Johnson, Kathy Kirby, and DJ Barry Alldis** Just some of the stars who taped their own Radio Luxembourg shows.

TONY ATKINSON – MAN OF MYSTERY

One might expect a that printer who arranged the content of hundreds of magazines, including the commissioning photographers to take "shots" of the rich and famous might have a handful of "happy snaps" with the odd personality, but that doesn't appear to be the case. Trolling through thousands of "Pop Weekly" and the Presley archives we were only able to find one.

And the picture above was taken at an Elvis Presley Fan Function at the Palais de Congres in Versailles, Paris in 1971 arranged by Jean Marc Gargiulo president of the "Treat Me Nice" EPFC of France and hosted by Radio Luxembourg DJ Peter Aldersley.

It was during this visit to Paris that the man who was known simply as Anthony aka Oberleutnant Anton Heidelberg took my father around Paris showing him the where the brothels use to be that he frequented including the

Chabanais. Between 1880 and 1914, Paris was the world capital of pleasures. All the pleasures … A time – the Belle Epoque! – that will know that its peak during the International Exhibition of 1900, where the French capital became a symbol of art of living and luxury. At the Belle Epoque, there were no fewer than 224 brothels in Paris, and a hundred in 1946, when houses off ill repute were closed by the French Government. Unlike other European cities, where prostitution was also tolerated, the sex in Paris was more class. Healthier first, with girls weekly checked by doctors, and appreciated for its "cocottes" meticulously chosen for its aristocratic and bourgeois clientele. With the German occupation of France from 1940 - 1944, WWII made the proprietors extremely wealthy.

Behind the picture of this fickle and dizzy 1900s Paris was another reality. In working-class neighbourhoods where people hid behind authorised brothels, sometimes ticket in the hand, waiting to enjoy the pleasures of a prostitute who could endure up to 60 tricks a day.

Paris from the 1900s onwards was made for love, lovers, mistresses, gigolos, and fetish fun and paying for it was an acceptable trade in the delights of fornication.

So, why were there no pictures of Tony? His stepson Charles has no pictures, not even passports, or wedding photographs. His British military ID we assume was destroyed when he became an Oberleutnant, as too would have been his fake German papers when he was accepted by the Maquis. There were no dog tags either. When he worked at BBC Monitoring in Reading there could have been a picture ID document but that was no doubt handed in when he left the service.

It has been said by those who worked with him that they thought Tony romanced about his past, but the stories he told me and my dad were so detailed and verifiable, it must be concluded, that much, if not all of what he told us, the majority of facts in this work are thought by me to be truthful. For my part I was in the bar when

Mandy Rice Davies told us to "drink up and fuck off!" I was there during our negotiations with Radio Luxembourg, and I have done everything possible from my end to confirm many of his adventures.

I am enamoured by this story of a printer who did so much during and after the war with no thought of celebrity for himself. Tony Atkinson was an amiable, genuine, kind, and thoughtful person who was my friend. I only wished that he had told me more, though this anonymity might hide other aspects of his military life. Let's get one thing straight, he was able to pass himself off as Oberleutnant Anton Heidelberg without hindrance or danger. His personality and charm were so believable that no one in the German Army thought it necessary to question too much the validity of his rank.

With so many German Soldiers in Paris there was always a chance that Tony would be captured, imprisoned, or even shot, but his confidence convinced everyone.

TODD SLAUGHTER PRODUCTIONS

When the first communications satellite was launched in 1962. I, like everyone else, was fascinated that we could see on our TVs live pictures relayed from the USA by Telstar. It was an orbiting satellite which meant that the line-of-site from the transmitting dish to the receiving dish was just 22 minutes during each revolution of the of the earth. British scientist, television presenter, under sea explorer, and space fiction writer (2001 A Space Odessey) Arthur C Clark calculated that the exact position for a communications satellite to be positioned over the equator to travel in sync with the orbit of the earth was 22,236 miles above the earth.

I saw an opportunity for Elvis to appear live on TV across the UK and Europe from the USA by satellite and I launched my "Elvis Via Telstar" campaign and to give the idea more umph I devised a training name of Todd Slaughter Production. It had three staff members: Me, myself, and I.

I wrote letters about my Elvis Via Telstar campaign in Elvis Monthly, Pop Weekly, NME, and Disc. I even got the idea announced on the Teen & Twenty Disc Club shows on Radio Luxembourg. I started to receive daily bundles of mail from Elvis Fans anxious to get involved so we launched a petition to encourage Colonel Parker to consider the opportunity. RCA product was distributed in the UK by the Decca Record Company, and my suggestion was having such an impact in the business press that in April 1963 I was invited into the director's dining room overlooking the River Thames located within their HQ at 9 Albert Embankment, London SE1 to meet the big boss man of the company Sir Edward Lewis. He said that unofficially he could not get involved because Decca was only the licensee of Elvis Presley's RCA product, but he suggested that I keep knocking on the door of Radio Luxembourg, as it was an international broadcaster across the continent of Europe.

When the first communications satellite was launched in 1962. I, like everyone else, was fascinated that we could see on our TVs live pictures relayed from the USA by Telstar. It was an orbiting satellite which meant that the line-of-site from the transmitting dish to the receiving dish was just 22 minutes during each revolution of the of the earth. British scientist, television presenter, under sea explorer, and space fiction writer (2001 A Space Odessey) Arthur C Clark calculated that the exact position for a communications satellite to be positioned over the equator to travel in sync with the orbit of the earth was 22,236 miles above the earth.

I thought that Elvis could and should appear live from the USA by satellite and I launched my "Elvis Via Telstar" campaign and to give the idea more umph I devised a training name of Todd Slaughter Production. It had three staff members: Me, myself, and I. I wrote letters about my Elvis Via Telstar campaign in Elvis Monthly, Pop Weekly, NME, and Disc. I even got the idea announced on the Teen & Twenty Disc Club shows on Radio Luxembourg.

I started to receive daily bundles of mail from Elvis Fans anxious to get involved so we launched a petition to encourage Colonel Parker to consider the opportunity. RCA product was distributed in the UK by the Decca Record Company, and my suggestion was having such an impact in the business press that in April 1963 I was invited into the director's dining room overlooking the River Thames located within their HQ at 9 Albert Embankment, London SE1 to meet the big boss man of the company Sir Edward Lewis. He said that unofficially he could not get involved because Decca was only the licensee of Elvis Presley's RCA product, but he suggested that I keep knocking on the door of Radio Luxembourg, as it was an international broadcaster across the continent of Europe.

Decca's sponsored radio programmes on 208 were hosted by an eccentric Yorkshire man called Jimmy Savile. Even the mention of "Savile" these days in an anathema, but in the 1960s this new not-so-quite "young" kid on the block quickly established himself as one of the big four DJs on British radio, the others being Alan Freeman, Pete Murray, and David Jacobs.

His gregarious persona quickly launched him onto TV, plus he met Elvis and Colonel Parker twice presenting him with gold and silver record sales awards. In the meantime, I had meetings with television executive Elkan Allen from Associated Rediffusion and contact was made with ABC and NBC to see if such a project was commercially viable.

It took a decade for Presley to complete his movie contract deals and return to live entertainment, but eventually Colonel Parker put together a deal. So, ten years later 4 September 1972 when Radio

Luxembourg DJ Tony Prince and I met Elvis for the first time, a press conference at the Las Vegas Hilton was called to announce that Elvis Presley would star live in a global telecast from Honolulu to over a predicted television audience more than one billion. The NBC show "Aloha from Hawaii" was broadcast live via satellite to audiences in Asia and Oceania on 14 January 1973. The show was presented with a delay in Europe. In the United States, to avoid a programming conflict with "Super Bowl VII" and MGM's "Elvis on Tour" which was playing in cinemas at the time, NBC opted to air a ninety-minute television special of the concert on 4 April.

Some years later in 1987 when discussing "Aloha from Hawaii" and taking in an interview for my *Satellite TV News* magazine with the then controller of BBC TV, Bill Cotton asked me what I thought would be the next global event the corporation should relay live. I answered, "The Hajj - this sacred journey, is undertaken by millions of Muslims It has never been seen live on TV." It took some years to arrange, and it was a cooperation between the BBC, Arabsat and Luxembourg's SES company.

Within my Elvis bubble apart from Tony Atkinson there were many industry people affected by the brutality of the Nazi regime. Colonel Parker who had immigrated to the USA on his third attempt in the summer of 1929 heard that the RMS Carinthia ship that he sailed on from Liverpool to Boston was sunk by a German torpedo in 1940 and his sister was raped in Breda, Holland in 1942 by a member od the Waffen SS. Freddy Bienstock, Elvis' music publisher was born to a Jewish family in Switzerland on April 24, 1923, and relocated to Vienna with his family when he was three-years old. After the Anschluss, he emigrated to the United States in 1938, just before the outbreak of World War II, with his brother Johnny

Bienstock, who later founded Big Top Records. The family ended up settling in New Jersey after his parents came to the U.S. in 1939. His other family members perished in Auschwitz.

Born in Postdam, Germany, Henri Lewin (pictured here with 208's Tony Prince and Todd Slaughter fled with his family in 1939 with the rise of Nazi Germany. His other family member died in the gas chambers of the concentration camps. He first worked for Hilton Hotels in Shanghai, China, before arriving in San Francisco in 1947. He landed a job as a busboy at The Fairmont Hotel, and where he was able to climb up the management ladder for the next 17 years before rejoining Hilton Hotels. Heinz "Henri" Lewin is best known for his 13-year tenure as a high-profile executive running the Las Vegas Hilton and Flamingo Hilton and as a principal of the first management team to run the Sands. Lewin's belief that Las Vegas could become a major destination. site, with good restaurants, fine rooms and large conventions, and superstar entertainers, especially Elvis put him out front in the area's history. He arrived in Las Vegas in 1972 from San Francisco after being appointed executive vice president in charge of Hilton Hotels Corp.'s gaming interests in Las Vegas having joined the company in 1964 as a protege of Hilton Hotels founder, Conrad Hilton.

2024 was certainly a year of landmark anniversaries. It is 90 years since Radio Luxembourg started regular English language programming on 1 January 1934, and eighty years since the Normandy landings and associated airborne operations the Allied invasion of Normandy in France. Codenamed "Operation Neptune", and often referred to as D-Day, it was the largest seaborne invasion in history. The operation began the liberation of France, and the rest of Western Europe, and laid the foundations of the Allied victory on the Western Front.

70 years ago, Elvis Presley recorded "That's All Right (Mama)" which when released in the summer of 1954 was deemed to be the true Genesis of a popular music culture that resulted internationally into a commercial powerhouse for the recording industry. The 60th anniversary of what was to be the spearhead of an armada of offshore broadcasters when Radio Caroline anchored of the Essex

coast and turned on, for the first time, its "tower of power" transmitter over Easter 1964.

50 years ago, ABBA won the Eurovision Song Contest held in Brighton, England and forever changed the dimension and content of the world's largest TV shopwindow for new talent, the BBC show up to then had been something of a bland production. 1974 was also a year of domestic troubles in the UK with a miners' strike, a three-day working week due to fuel and energy shortages, TV closing down at 10.30pm to save electricity and a plethora of IRA bombings across the UK. The 50th anniversary of troubles and strife, including Stateside with the Watergate Political Scandal with the only highlight being the discovery of the Wombles on Wimbledon Common and Mud Topping the Christmas Charts with "Lonely this Christmas". 1984 and another Miners Strike, this time thwarted by the Iron Lady Prime Minister Margaret Thatcher. The Apple Mac computer was launched as too was Richard Branson's Virgin Atlantic Airways. Also 40 years ago, Marvin Gaye was shot dead by his father, Ghostbusters the movie was a box office smash, Crack Cocaine was being sold as a new street drug in LA, HIV was identified, and Britain returned the sovereignty of Hong Kong to China. "Do They Know it's Christmas" sold millions of copies with proceeds going to Bob Geldof's Ethiopian Famine Charity. For me personally 2024 - the anniversary some thirty years ago of my heart transplant at Papworth Hospital. And for everyone, me included, Amazon was launched in 1994.

8 May 2025, sees the 80th anniversary of the end of WWII in Europe, November 2025 Elvis Presley signed with RCA orchestrated by Colonel Parker, oil shortages stopped the manufacture of vinyl records and the following month sees by 80th.

I was at the Luxembourg Embassy in London in 2017 for a reception of Tony Prince's "The Royal Ruler and the Railway DJ" when at the party afterwards I bumped into DJ Andy Peebles. He said, "Hey Todd we've got something in common. I recorded an interview the day before John Lennon was shot dead in New York, and you were the last person to be commercially filmed and photographed with Elvis before he died." "Yes, I was at Indianapolis Airport 26 June 1977 to meet Elvis and receive an award for services rendered, just before he performed his last ever concert.

TODD SLAUGHTER

THE NIGHT HAS A THOUSAND SPIES - PLUS ONE

On the morning of the 80th anniversary of D – Day (6 June 2024) I received an anonymous package containing three medals with the compliments of the Under Secretary of State for Defence. The France and German Star, the Defence Medal for Brave Conduct and the War Medal 1939 – 1945. I had tried to find out just what my birth mother, PTE Betty Doreen Gitsham, was doing in Belgium during WW II. Listed as an anti-aircraft gunner such a title is a bit odd as women in the ATS were not allowed to fire munitions. I had spoken to several people in the War Office, but no one would respond to my questioning apart from saying that under the rules of the Official Secrets Act they couldn't say what she did, though they confirmed that she was at an advantage as she spoke fluent French. "Was it covert?" There was no response. So, was she a Spy? They did say that there was chance that my unnamed GI birth father, was killed during a clean-up operation after the Battle of the Bulge and if so, would be buried along with Gen. Patton in the American Cemetery in Luxembourg.

IN CONCLUSION It is with thanks to the picture source providers and the people who have supported me over the past years with particular reference to this work.: Lee Docherty (Under Secretary of State for Defence – Armed Forces), Lord Michael Howard, Peter Thurnham MP (dec.), Sir Roger Gale MP, Lord Lew Grade (dec.), Lord Michael Grade, Sir Tim Rice, Sir Bill Cotton (dec.) and Colonel Tom Parker (dec.). Elvis Presley (dec.), Alvin Stardust (dec.), Les Gray (dec.), Freddie Starr (dec.), Reginald Bosanquet (dec.), Ray Dorset, Simon Withington, Tony Prince, Mark Wesley, Paul Burnett, Mike Read, Don Wardell, Stuart Henry (dec.), Emperor Rosko, Rodney Collins, Alan Keen (dec.), Alex Dyke, Kid Jensen, Bob Stewart (dec.), Tommy Vance (dec.), David Hamilton, Roger Day,

David Lloyd, Paul Robey, Kamlesh Purohit, Bob Badwal, Victoria Molloy (dec.), Carolina Reinertz (Samsa), Sally Molloy, Ayoub Haciane, Albert Hand (dec.), Dave Kaye, Bill Kenwright (dec.), Steve Wright (dec.), Marty Wilde, Adrian Tredeschi, Candace Rose, Lee Jackson, Dr Jayan Parameshwar, Dr Alex Todd, Glenda Pickering, Joanne and Mike, many more friends plus my family, and Tony Atkinson (dec.)

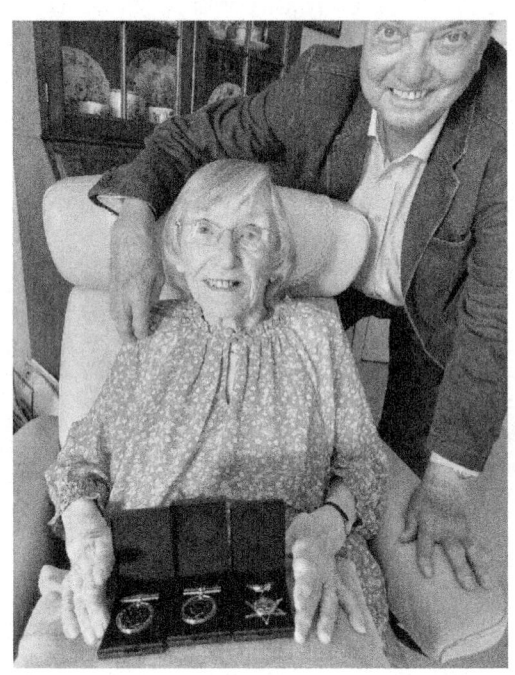

My "Aunty Sheila", who was the youngest sister of my birth mother Betty Doreen Gitsham who died 9 June 1995, passed away in March 2025. Sheila Lapthorn is seen here with me and my late mother's Medals. She never knew what her sister did during WWII and was so proud to learn of her courage.

Printed in Great Britain
by Amazon

59376075R00116